Following Jesus in the Holy Land

Pathways of Discipleship through Advent and Lent

— STEPHEN W. NEED —

Sacristy
Press

Sacristy Press
PO Box 612, Durham, DH1 9HT

www.sacristy.co.uk

First published in 2019 by Sacristy Press, Durham

Sacristy Limited, registered in England & Wales, number 7565667

British Library Cataloguing-in-Publication Data
A catalogue record for the book is available from the British Library

ISBN 978-1-78959-041-8

In gratitude for
St George's College
Jerusalem

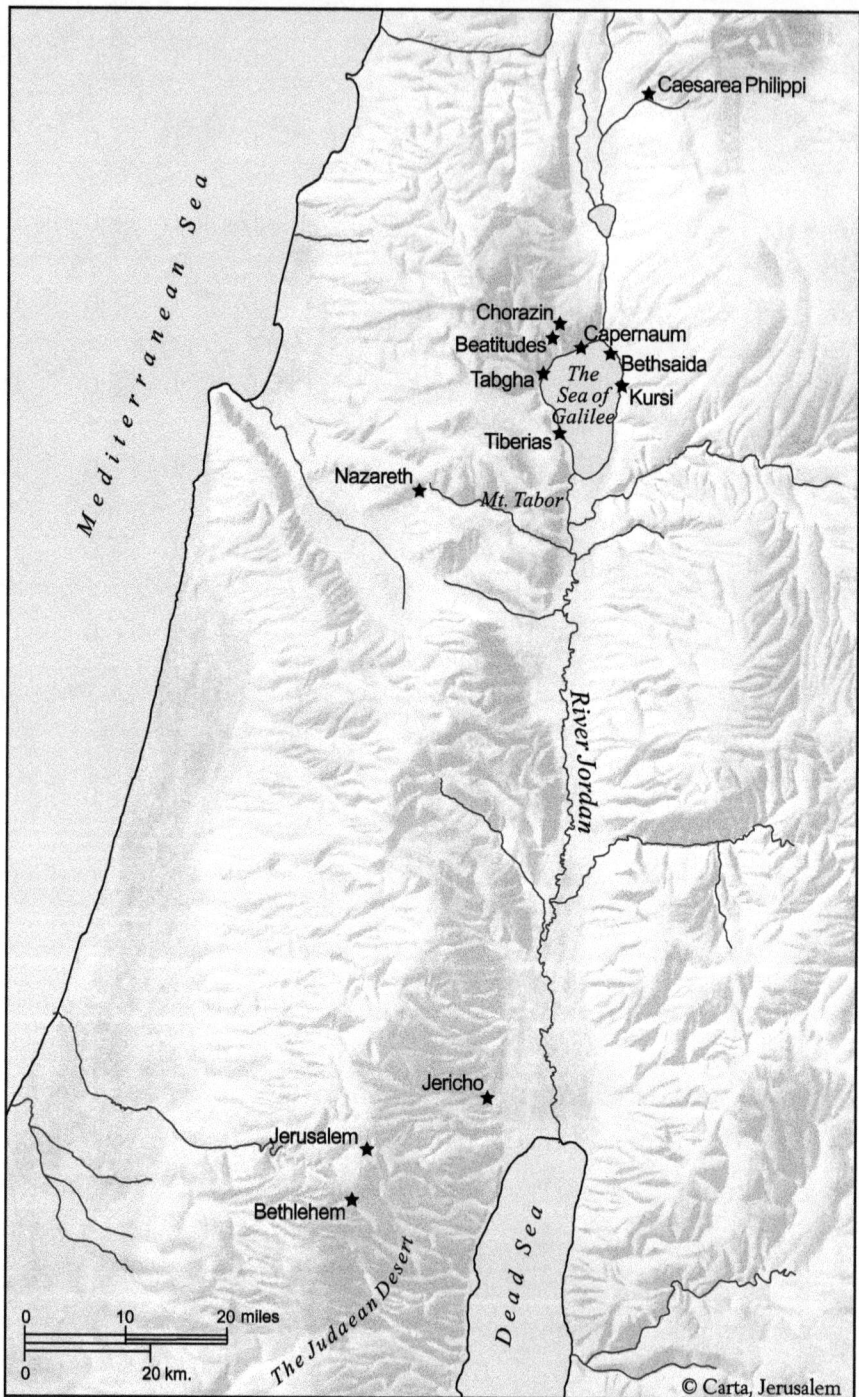

Caesarea Philippi

Mediterranean Sea

Chorazin
Beatitudes
Tabgha
Capernaum
Bethsaida
Kursi
The Sea of Galilee
Tiberias

Nazareth
Mt. Tabor

River Jordan

Jericho

Jerusalem

Bethlehem

The Judaean Desert

Dead Sea

0   10   20 miles
0   20 km.

© Carta, Jerusalem

Preface

This book has been written to help stimulate individual and group study during the Church's seasons of Advent and Lent. Using places in the Holy Land as lenses through which to look at Christian faith and life, it is effectively a course book for the main part of the Church's year. It will take you on a journey to some of the key places in the Holy Land and through some of the key parts of the Gospels. You don't have to have been to the Holy Land; you will travel there in your imagination. If you have been or are planning to go, the book will help you reflect on your experience or get ready. It will be ideal for group or personal use at church or at home during the lead-up to Christmas and Easter.

A kind of "armchair pilgrimage" to the Holy Land, the book arose out of several years actually living there and experiencing the holy places as powerful aids to re-imagining the gospel narratives as well as the seasons of the Church's year and various stages in Christian life. Viewing the gospel narratives and events through the places associated with them in the Holy Land brings the texts and their meanings to life in a powerful and vivid way. There's a chapter a week here throughout the two seasons.[1]

The title of the book draws attention to the overriding theme of discipleship and the challenge of following Jesus. As you look through the lens of the Holy Land, and particular lenses in each chapter, you will discover new aspects of Jesus' life, ministry, death and resurrection as found in the four Gospels. As each of the ten chapters unfolds and the ten places are introduced and discussed so you will travel through ten stages in Christian life, from experiencing God at the beginning of Advent to the resurrection life of Easter.

Working within this framework, you will become aware of an overall theological scheme based on Christology or who Jesus is for Christians today. First, you will be led into thinking of him in terms of the Jerusalem Temple, as the place where God dwells. Then, you are invited to think of

Bethlehem and God stooping in Jesus' birth. Nazareth is the place where Jesus grew in wisdom and is your lens for doing the same. Finally, for Advent, you are asked to think about Jesus' baptism in the River Jordan and how that is related to your own baptism. In the first part of the book, between Advent and Christmas, you will notice an overall basic pattern: the presence of God and your response to it.

Part Two is for Lent and invites you to look through more lenses. This section begins in the Judaean Desert with the experience of God in solitude and stripping bare. The second week takes you to the Sea of Galilee and the context of Jesus' ministry, focusing on his teaching about the kingdom of God. Caesarea Philippi in the Golan Heights confronts you with the major decision about whether to follow Jesus seriously to the end. And then Mount Tabor, the mountain of transfiguration, draws you into the idea of playing a part in transfiguring the world. The Last Supper and its meaning are glimpsed through looking at the likely location of the meal in Jerusalem. And the perfect ending at Easter is the Church of the Holy Sepulchre in Jerusalem, prompting you to think about Jesus' death and resurrection. You will notice that in the second part of the book the basic pattern laid down in Part One is deepened: God's presence in Jesus and your lifestyle as a disciple.

Through the Holy Places of the Holy Land, this book paints a picture of Jesus as the one in whom God dwells and as the one who gives Christians an example of a life lived for God. It incorporates both belief and practice or Christology and ethics. Each chapter provides interesting historical, archaeological and biblical material as well as a reflection for contemporary Christian faith and life. Biblical texts, psalms and hymns for worship, activities, questions for discussion, bibliographies and endnotes all enable you to take your study and reflection even further.

I am grateful to the staff at Sacristy Press for their help and encouragement in bringing this book to publication and to Bishop Stephen Platten for reading through an early draft.

I hope you will find this journey through the Holy Land stimulating and informative as well as useful—a possible way of thinking about and living Christian faith, not just in Advent and Lent but in every season.

Stephen W. Need
Essex, March 2019

Contents

Part One: Advent to Christmas

CHAPTER 1

Jerusalem: Jesus the "New Temple"

We begin in Jerusalem on the Mount of Olives looking west across the Kidron Valley. A scramble of golden limestone buildings, ancient and modern, comes into focus in the bright sunlight revealing a Middle Eastern walled city in the desert. In the background, new high-rise hotels provide a contrasting skyline. Hills and valleys surround the broad picture. Churches, synagogues and mosques provide the contours. In the foreground, you can see over three thousand years of history at a glance. This is the Old City of Jerusalem.

As you look more closely, your eye is drawn immediately to the striking golden Dome of the Rock. Standing on a stone platform easily discernible and the size of twelve football fields, its octagonal structure exudes bright blue and green colours. Other buildings and archways nestle close to it. There's an overwhelming sense of presence, as if something has come from outer space and settled on earth. The atmosphere exudes history and eternity, mystery and enigma, as one reality seems to break in upon another. It's as if heaven and earth have met here in this strange location, in a stunning encounter.

None of this is surprising when you come to know the place. For the Jews it's the Temple Mount, for the Arabs the Noble Sanctuary. Here the ancient temples of Judaism stood for over a thousand years. And here the colourful Muslim shrine still stands. There's no wonder the place is unusual: it's where God has been experienced for millennia; where sacrifice was offered thousands of times; and where the Call to Prayer has rung out for centuries. From the Mount of Olives, you're looking at a God-inhabited, God-soaked and God-trodden landscape; a sacred space where God was said to make his dwelling and where he was thought to live on earth.

After a few minutes' reflection, we're off down the mountain road into the Kidron Valley below. There are churches scattered about and cars trying to get along a narrow street. On one side a huge graveyard appears, the resting place of Jews waiting to enter the Holy City at the end of time. On the other side, a wall conceals the Russian Orthodox Church of St Mary Magdalene, its dazzling, golden, onion-shaped domes shining in the sun. Below, in the floor of the Kidron, is the Garden of Gethsemane, where Jesus prayed the night before he died.

We continue to make our way, following the road around outside the city wall and then up through the Dung Gate into the Old City itself. After queueing near the Wailing Wall, a ramp takes us up through military security onto the platform of Herod's Temple. We're now actually standing on the plateau we saw from the Mount of Olives. In Jesus' day this was the Temple Precinct with columns and gates all around. Today, political tension is tangible as religious ideologies compete for pre-eminence. Even so, an overwhelming sense of the presence of God persists.

The Jerusalem Temple

In this first chapter we take the Temple Mount in Jerusalem as a lens through which to look at Jesus. We think about where God dwells and where God might be found in our own lives today. In John's Gospel, Jesus himself speaks of his body as the temple (2:21), suggesting a way of thinking of Jesus as God's dwelling place. In this first week, we focus on the Jerusalem Temple and then on Jesus as the "new temple".

First of all, let us look at the Jerusalem Temples which stood on the platform still visible today from the Mount of Olives. Over a thousand-year period, two main temples stood on this site. Our primary interest is in the Temple that Jesus knew and visited more than once for major Jewish festivals. Started by Zerubbabel in the sixth century BC it was extended by Herod the Great from 19 BC onwards and is the setting in the Gospels for the famous incident known as the "Cleansing of the Temple". It is known as the Second Temple. According to the Jewish historian Josephus this massive building was constructed in white marble reflecting the bright sunlight and dazzling onlookers.[2] There was silver and gold decoration and the impact of the whole building would have stunned onlookers on the Mount of Olives opposite.

Herod's Temple complex consisted of a series of graded courts leading from an outer court up to the Holy of Holies, from the earthly to the heavenly, from the human to the divine, from time to eternity. First, there was the Court of the Gentiles into which both Jews and Gentiles could go. This was the largest area, occupying most of the space seen on the Temple Mount today. In this area Jesus confronted the sellers and money changers. But Gentiles could go no further and an important wall separated this court from the next one, the Court of the Women. The wall displayed notices in Latin and Greek, warning Gentiles to stay away on pain of death. The Court of the Women was open to all Jews but women could go no further. Then followed the Court of the Israelites open to all male Jews but only priests could go further into the Court of the Priests.

After this was the Temple Court which housed the Holy of Holies, the sacred inner sanctum where God himself dwelt. Only the High Priest could go into the inner space and he only once a year on the Day of Atonement. It was in front of this inner sanctum that the "veil of the Temple" hung, the curtain separating the inner from the outer, the heavenly from the earthly. Thus, the structure of the Temple was a graded hierarchical series of stages before reaching the ultimate holy place. Herod's Temple, the so-called "Second Temple", was considered so holy that it was thought of literally as God's dwelling place on earth. It was destroyed by the Romans in 70 AD.[3]

The other temple, the First Temple, was the Temple of Solomon. This stood on a much smaller platform in the same area a thousand years earlier. There are no remains today but we know it was different in design from Herod's Temple. A courtyard surrounded the main building which had three sections: the porch, the sanctuary and the inner sanctum. In the courtyard were the furnishings for sacrifice. The inner sanctum of this temple contained the tablets of the Ten Commandments in the Ark of the Covenant brought up from the desert by the Israelites. In the desert the Ark had been the sign of God's presence with his people. In Solomon's Temple the Ark now also symbolized the divine presence. Although we don't know exactly what the Ark looked like, it was a golden box with two cherubim on the lid or mercy seat and four larger ones on the corners.

Whatever the differences between the First and Second Temples, they were both seen as God's ultimate dwelling place on earth.

In Jewish thinking, the temples in Jerusalem were the place where heaven and earth met. The specific purpose was blood sacrifice. In offering the blood of an animal to God, the Jews maintained they were giving back to God what he had created. The many types of sacrifice are detailed in the Book of Leviticus (1–7). Their purpose was to bridge the gap that had opened up between humanity and God and to mend the broken relationship. The sacrifices were carried out continuously, with the offering of a great deal of blood. As well as being the house of God, therefore, the Jerusalem Temples were houses of sacrifice and atonement.

The Old Testament scholar Margaret Barker likens the experience of God at Solomon's Temple to Jacob's encounter with God at Bethel in Genesis 28:10–17. Of Bethel Jacob says, "How awesome is this place! This is none other than the house of God, and this is the gate of heaven (v. 17)."[4] This was also true of Herod's Temple in the time of Jesus: it was the gate of heaven, the gate to God's house, the entrance to the place where God could be known, experienced and worshipped.

Jesus in the Temple

In one of the most dramatic events in the Gospels, Jesus enters the Jerusalem Temple and overthrows the tables of money changers and those selling animals. Usually known as the "Cleansing of the Temple", the incident is in all four Gospels, and New Testament scholars believe it has a strong basis in history. It certainly has a strong theological significance. In Matthew, Mark and Luke, the story occurs towards the end of the Gospel, giving a dramatic start to the last days of Jesus' life (Matthew 21:12–17; Mark 11:15–19; Luke 19:45–48). But in John's Gospel it occurs near the beginning, adding a flavour to everything else Jesus says and does (2:13–22).

As we have seen, the temple setting is significant. The more immediate context is the moneychangers and the buying and selling of animals for sacrifice. These would almost certainly have occupied space in the huge Court of the Gentiles. It is Jesus' encounter with these that forms the pivot of this story. All the accounts tell us that Jesus enters the temple and drives out the buyers and sellers, and all apart from Luke tell us that he overturned their tables. There is then the quotation that seems to give the event its meaning: "Is it not written, 'My house shall be called a house of prayer for all the nations'? But you have made it a den of robbers" (Mark 11:17).

The longest version of the incident comes in John. Here Jesus makes a whip of cords and drives out the moneychangers. And when the Jews ask him what sign he has for doing this, he answers, "Destroy this temple, and in three days I will raise it up" (2:19). Only John's Gospel includes the prophecy of the destruction of the temple, and only he comments that the temple Jesus is referring to is his own body (2:21). As we shall see shortly, this detail is of major importance.

The incident in the temple is clearly one of Jesus' main prophetic actions, but it has had many interpretations.[5] On the face of it, it looks as though Jesus is challenging the temple system of sacrifice. His confrontation is with those who are selling animals for sacrifice and changing money to enable people to buy an animal. It is often thought that Jesus is acting here against the system of sacrifice and in favour of a pure religion of the heart. Others have read the whole event as indicating that Jesus was in some way against the temple, like the Essenes of Qumran and others. In this view, he is inaugurating a new religious movement. But none of this seems likely given Jesus' own Jewishness and his behaviour in the rest of the Gospels. He might, of course, be a radicalizer objecting against the corruption of the temple system of sacrifice rather than being against the temple as such.

But there is another more likely interpretation. In overturning the tables of the moneychangers, Jesus is demonstrating his own role as a prophetic figure ushering in the last days. In the Judaism of Jesus' day it was believed that at the end of time the temple would be renewed and God's purposes would be carried out for both Jews and Gentiles through the establishment of a new temple (see e.g. Zechariah 14:20–21; Malachi 3:1). The idea that Jesus himself is the new temple arises out of this. His action in the Court of the Gentiles is symbolic of God's new relation with his people, and in the new context he himself replaces the old temple as the place where God is known. This is the line of thought in John's Gospel when we are told that Jesus was speaking of his own body when he spoke of the destruction of the temple.

This theology of Jesus as the "new temple" can also be found in the Letter to the Hebrews and in the Book of Revelation. In Hebrews, Jesus is the high priest of the temple who has passed behind the curtain and opened up the way between humanity and God. The Gospels already use this image when they say that at the time of his death "the curtain of the temple was torn in two" (Mark 15:38). Jesus is also the last of the priests offering the last of the sacrifices (Hebrews 9:11–14) and is himself said to be the temple curtain (10:20). In the Book of Revelation the symbolism of the temple is intertwined with that of the lamb and of the city of Jerusalem itself (5:6–14; 11:19; 21:2). The lamb is the symbol of Jesus, but in Chapter 21 there is a vision of the New Jerusalem coming down from heaven and there is no temple in the city, "for its temple is the Lord God the Almighty and the Lamb" (21:22). Now, God himself coupled with Jesus the lamb is the real temple. In all of this, temple imagery is used to show that for Christians Jesus opens up the way to God and is now the new dwelling place of God.

And so, the real thrust of the incident in the temple is not that it somehow "cleanses the temple" from its corruption but that Jesus announces the coming of a new age when the temple will be renewed and replaced. Although there are different emphases among the writers, the New Testament shows us quite clearly that Jesus is now the real temple, the old one has passed away. He is the renewed temple expected at the end of time. In this picture, the Jerusalem Temple works as a powerful metaphor for Jesus himself. He is the one in whom God's presence now dwells and the place where God may now be encountered, worshipped and known. And he is the one in whom the sacrifice for sin will now take place.

This "temple theology", therefore, refocuses our understanding of Jesus and in Advent helps us ask where we find God in our own lives. It helps us look again at the life, death and resurrection of Jesus and see in them the dwelling place of God.[6]

Jesus is the temple

With this discussion of the Jerusalem Temple and Jesus' actions in the Temple in mind, we turn now to our own situation today: Where might Christians look for God now? Where might we expect to find or experience God? In Advent, at the beginning of the Church's year, it is particularly important to ask this question. And at a time when we are thinking of the coming of God into our own lives it's useful to focus on the image of the Jerusalem Temple and on Jesus as the new temple. Just as the Jews of Jesus' own day found God in the Temple, so we can find God through looking at Jesus now.

The question about where we find God usually receives varied and quite personal answers. For many people, especially churchgoers, the answer might be "in church during worship". That's often why people go to church, to get in touch with God and to get close to God. In searching for something beyond their everyday lives, people find what they're looking for in church. There is certainly a good case for saying that God should be experienced in church, for if he cannot be found there, where can he be found?

But there are those, churchgoers among them, who might experience God more in nature, in the garden or in a sunset.[7] After all, is God not the creator of all things? And as part of that, others might say they experience God in art, music and architecture, and in the creative processes of life. A stunning Caravaggio painting, a Mozart symphony, a glorious cathedral like Chartres or Lincoln carries the human spirit up to God. In poetry and in film, in sport and in photography, and in every kind of creative process, God can be found. And we might wish to say that we find God most of all in our families and in all the goodness of human community. Indeed, for Christians this brings us back to the church and all that it is intended to be.

But there is more for Christians than the God found in nature, art, family and friends, however important these might be. People of other faiths and people of no particular faith find God in nature and even though that is fundamental to Christian faith it is not its defining feature. It is, rather, Jesus who is the focus for Christians. We see God in Jesus' life, death and resurrection, in what he did, taught and stood for. It is in his particular life that we see God dwelling, just as the Jews saw him dwelling in the Jerusalem Temple. The experience of God in other places is filtered through Jesus. It might be difficult to be sure about some of the historical detail of Jesus' life but the gospel picture characterized by humility, compassion and healing is fundamental here.[8]

The notion that God dwells in Jesus is, of course, the beginning of what we call "Christology". This is concerned with who Jesus was and is and how we are to think of God dwelling in him. From the very beginning Christians have spoken of Jesus as their saviour, they have called him Messiah, Son of God and Son of Man and have acknowledged him as Lord. For centuries they have used the idea of the Word or *logos* of God dwelling in Jesus. In John's Gospel, Jesus is the place where "the Word became flesh and lived among us" (1:14), hinting already at the idea that he is another temple or dwelling place of God. And in 1 Corinthians Jesus is "the power of God and the wisdom of God", also indicating God dwelling in Jesus (1:24). The councils of the Church and the many controversies of the early centuries struggled with finding the right language to articulate how God had dwelt in Jesus. The language of "incarnation" became central: God was "embodied" or "enfleshed" in Jesus. This had a complex Greek philosophical background but at its heart was the idea that God dwelt in Jesus in a very special way.

The idea that God dwelt in Jesus as he dwelt in the Jerusalem Temple doesn't yet say everything there is to say about Jesus but it makes a significant move in the right direction. Far from being a religion that saw God dwelling in a building, however important, or in nature or art, Christianity from the beginning saw God dwelling in a person and in a particular life lived. It acknowledged that in the life, death and resurrection of Jesus something particular about God had been seen. And it saw that Jesus, like the temple, had been the place where people could find God and come into his presence. Paul certainly knew this when he wrote in his second Letter to the Corinthians that, "in Christ God was reconciling the world to himself" (5:19).

Conclusion

We began on the Mount of Olives in Jerusalem looking at the Temple Mount or Noble Sanctuary and walking through the Kidron Valley up onto the platform to the very place where ancient Jews believed God lived and where people have experienced his presence in one form or another for centuries. This special place recalls the temples that stood here for a thousand years, the place of God's dwelling. The temples were the "gate of heaven", the way through into God's presence. And there's still a strong sense of that presence on the Mount today.

In the New Testament, Jesus himself is thought of as the temple or the place of God's dwelling. He himself is the "gate of heaven". Something about God's very presence is shown in Jesus' life, death and resurrection. The incident in the Gospels often known as the "Cleansing of the Temple" has been read in a number of different ways, but it should most probably be thought of as Jesus ushering in a new age, when the temple would be renewed. Instead of a renewed building, the New Testament sees Jesus himself as the new temple, and we can still think of him in that way now.

During Advent turn your mind to God's dwelling among us and ask the basic question "where do you find God?" You might answer this in different ways at different times. But in the end, the presence of God is surely more than a beautiful sunset, a wonderful piece of music or a special building. It is seen in a life lived: the life of Jesus whose particular way of living for others shows you something different about what God is like. The idea of the temple as God's house is a lens used of Jesus, so that God's presence can now be seen in a person. And Jesus is also a lens through which we can look at ourselves and gauge our responses to him.

Things to do

Bible study passages
- Genesis 28:10–17
- 1 Kings 8:1–13
- John 2:13–22

Worship

- Psalms: 24; 84; 122
- Hymns: Christ is made the sure foundation; Bright the vision that delighted.

Activities

- Visit a place of worship (church, synagogue, mosque or another). What is your sense of God's presence there?
- Think of a particular person in whom you have found God's presence. Share experiences with your group.

Questions for discussion

- What do we know about the temple in Jerusalem at the time of Jesus?
- What does it mean to say that God "dwells" in Jesus?
- Discuss the places where you have found God especially present.

Further reading

Simon Goldhill, *The Temple of Jerusalem* (London: Profile Books, 2004).

Andrew D. Mayes, *Holy Land? Challenging Questions from the Biblical Landscape* (London: SPCK, 2011).

Tom Wright, *Simply Jesus: Who he was. What he did. Why it matters* (London: SPCK, 2011).

CHAPTER 2

Bethlehem: God Stooping

With the idea of God dwelling in "Jesus the new temple" we now travel five miles south of Jerusalem to Jesus' birthplace in Bethlehem. Along the busy road we pass through a kaleidoscope of buildings stretching out into modern Jerusalem. Then, we come to the Israeli separation wall where we pause and show passports. Aware that this can be a humiliating experience for locals, we pass through the wall into the famous "little town". Today it's a bustling Arab market town in the West Bank with a population of about 25,000. The feel inside Bethlehem is quite different from Jerusalem.

On the way in, we see shops, hotels, churches and mosques. We're in a separate enclave, less westernized and less economically prosperous. There are new buildings and developments but there's a strong feeling that we're now in a traditional Arab town. Bethlehem is famous for its olive wood and Mother of Pearl, and there are plenty of cafes, shops and restaurants for an Arabic coffee and baklava. Further into town we see local markets selling delicious food and colourful clothing. Once predominantly Christian, it's now mostly Muslim, many Christian families having left in recent years. What makes Bethlehem different, of course, is that it's the birthplace of Jesus, and so it's special to Christians and Muslims alike.

Wandering around Bethlehem is an eye-opening experience for visitors and pilgrims, and the place soon gets a grip on your imagination. But the main attraction is the Church of the Nativity in Manger Square. Marking the traditional birthplace of Jesus, it's been a place of pilgrimage, prayer and devotion for sixteen hundred years. Once on the square, we pick out the recently-cleaned stonework of the Church of the Nativity. Adjacent buildings are an Armenian monastery and the modern Roman

Catholic Church of St Catherine. Often covered with pilgrims, tourists and vendors, the piazza outside the church adjoins the square.

As we approach the church, we notice the most unusual entrance: the doorway into one of the greatest shrines of Christendom is unusually small and low. Can this really be the entrance? We stoop to get through. Bending low, we almost crawl, minding not to trip on a curb or bang our heads. We're nearly on the floor as we feel our way forward. And then the light changes. It's dark inside, making it quite difficult to see at first. As our eyes get accustomed to the new light, we realize we're in a very special place indeed. This is the entrance to the birthplace of Jesus! In this chapter this little doorway forms our second lens for Advent.

Where Jesus was born

The original church in Bethlehem built by Constantine the Great in the fourth century and the rebuild by Justinian in the sixth century both had very grand entrances. But sometime during the long Ottoman period (1517–1917) the small doorway you've just crawled through was put in. The practical reason was probably to keep out animals. But the contemporary pilgrim understanding of the door is our interest here: it's low to remind you that as you stoop to enter, so God also stooped to enter the world in the birth of Jesus. After all, this church is the Church of the Nativity and marks the incarnation, the birth of God into the world in the person of Jesus. For this reason, the small door of the church is often called the "door of humility".

The Church of the Nativity is an Orthodox church used by Greek, Armenian and Syrian Christians. Inside there are lights, lamps and mosaics as well as icons which are positioned on the iconostasis or screen at the high-altar end of the church. An important part of the theology and spirituality of the Orthodox Church, the icons depict the Trinity, Jesus, the Virgin Mary and the saints. In the sixth century the church must have been glorious, covered from floor to ceiling with colourful mosaics inside and out. Sadly, although the building often escaped attack, it suffered major damage from earthquakes which are common in the area. In recent years, the church has become a World Heritage Site, undergoing a major restoration in the last few years supported by the governments of several countries. The result is staggering, with the mosaics now gleaming as if they were brand new.

The overall significance of the church is important: it is a kind of "theology in stone" telling the story of Jesus' birth not only through marking the traditional place but also through the mediaeval wall mosaics. From the remains it is still possible to pick out some of the texts from the seven ecumenical councils of the Church through which early Christian doctrine was thrashed out.

The focal point of the church is the Cave of the Nativity. This is another very unusual place. Originally part of a complex of caves, it was gradually separated out and a church built over it. Today the cave lies below the high altar of the church. Pilgrims pass down a number of steps to enter what is a small chapel in the rock. Inside, there are two areas: one a small altar with the famous fourteen-pointed star underneath it marking the place of Jesus' birth. The number 14 reminds pilgrims of the three lots of fourteen generations in Matthew's genealogy of Jesus (1:1–17), as well as the numerical value of King David's name in Hebrew. The other location, marked by another altar and some lamps, marks the place where Jesus was laid in a manger. To kneel and pray in the Cave of the Nativity is a unique and incredibly moving experience.

The "door of humility" and the Cave of the Nativity in Bethlehem both speak of the stooping of God in the birth of Jesus. They remind anyone who enters that God did not come as a worldly king but as a humble human being. The church tells the story of who Jesus was and is for Christians. As pilgrims leave the cave and go back out of the door, they are mindful that the story of Jesus is one of humility and compassion, of lowliness and servanthood, of one whose life was given for others.

The idea of God stooping in the birth of Jesus, focused for us here by the Church of the Nativity in Bethlehem and the cave of Jesus' birth, is a fundamental part of Christianity and of the seasons of Advent and Christmas. What does the New Testament say about it?

Christmas stories

The birth of Jesus is one of the most important events in history. For Christians it is linked up to his life, death and resurrection. How are we to imagine Jesus' birth today? Most people know of it only through Nativity plays and Christmas carols such as "O little town of Bethlehem" and "Once in royal David's city". The popular version of the story usually includes the following: Mary and Joseph, and the angel Gabriel; Mary getting pregnant; the census taking them to Bethlehem; "no room at the inn"; the birth and lying the baby in a manger; shepherds and angels appearing; and the family fleeing to Egypt.

But how does all this relate to what we know about Jesus' birth from the New Testament and what were the real circumstances of his birth? There are some striking differences and some amazing surprises here! It is news to most people that the New Testament doesn't say much about the birth of Jesus. The earliest writer and one of the greatest, the apostle Paul, doesn't say anything about it at all. He does say that Jesus was "born of a woman, born under the law" (Galatians 4:4) and that Jesus was "descended from David according to the flesh" (Romans 1:3), but there's no mention of Bethlehem or anything that we know from the Christmas story. Paul seems not to have known or been interested in Jesus' birth. There's no mention of the birth in most of the other New Testament writers either and the earliest Gospel, Mark, says nothing about it. Even John's Gospel, perhaps the most theologically profound, and the one that tells us that "the Word became flesh" (1:14), says nothing about Jesus' birth in Bethlehem.[9]

It is only the Gospels of Matthew (1–2) and Luke (1–2) that tell us anything about Jesus' birth, and the two accounts are strikingly different.[10] Luke gives us most of what we know from the traditional story, but Matthew is the first in the New Testament and is probably older. By comparing the two accounts we can uncover what the main themes are. Matthew begins with a genealogy or family tree for Jesus, tracing his lineage back through three sets of fourteen generations (1:1–17). We then get the angel appearing to Joseph in a dream announcing the birth of Jesus (1:18–25) with the famous quotation from Isaiah about a virgin conceiving (v. 23). This is followed by the coming of the three Wise Men

(2:1–12) and the flight of the family to Egypt (2:13–15). Finally, there's the massacre of the children by King Herod (2:16–18) and the family's move to Nazareth (2:19–23). In Matthew, there are no shepherds or angels, and Joseph is the key character after Jesus. The main theme overall is that in the birth of this child God himself has come near. He is called "Emmanuel" or "God is with us" (1:23).

In Luke's Gospel, the story is very different, and it is this version that has influenced the account we usually get in Nativity plays and in church, although there are some differences here as well. Luke's account begins with a whole chapter on John the Baptist and his birth. This is not in Matthew but takes up half the material in Luke. After a literary dedication (1:1–4), John the Baptist's birth is recounted (1:5–25). Only after this do we find Jesus' birth announced. This time an angel appears to Mary (not Joseph as in Matthew) in the account which is often heard in churches at Christmas (1:26–38). Then there's the account of Mary visiting Elizabeth, mother of John the Baptist (1:39–45), followed by the *Magnificat* (1:46–56). The birth of John the Baptist (1:57–67) and the *Benedictus* (1:68–80) then follow.

It's only now in Luke that the birth of Jesus occurs with the shepherds and angels present (2:1–20). There are no Wise Men or Flight to Egypt (as in Matthew). It is also noteworthy that the traditional idea of there being "no room at the inn" isn't really in Luke, who in his original Greek is probably thinking not so much of an inn but the part of a cave (as it would have been in Judaea) in which human beings lived. There was no room in the human area (the *kataluma* as Luke says), so they laid him in the animal area in an eating trough (the *phatne*). This is the much more likely context of Jesus' birth, and though it shatters our traditional understanding, it is probably much closer to the original circumstances.

Following his birth and circumcision, Jesus is taken to the temple in Jerusalem for his presentation, and we hear the *Nunc Dimittis* from Simeon (2:21–39).

The scene then jumps to the only story we have about Jesus' childhood: when he is twelve years old he is taken to Jerusalem for Passover and ends up in the temple speaking with the teachers (2:41–52). In spite of the very different material in Luke, however, the overall theme is similar to Matthew: God has come near in Jesus who will be a saviour (2:11).

In the New Testament, then, the accounts of Jesus' birth differ from each other. They each contribute features that were later harmonized into one general account. In the second century an apocryphal Gospel known as the *Protevangelium of James* filled out the picture and later still the Gospel of Pseudo-Matthew added the ox and the ass (cf. Isaiah 1:3).[11] For centuries, the Christian imagination added other features to the Nativity story. Even so, there is an overriding sense in both Matthew and Luke, and indeed in later accounts, that in the birth of Jesus God came close in a particular and special way. Indeed, we might say that both Matthew and Luke stand in line in their accounts of Jesus' birth with the doorway to the Church of the Nativity in Bethlehem: in this birth, God "stooped" or came especially near to human beings.

God stoops down

Even though the story of Jesus' birth only occurs in the Gospels of Matthew and Luke in the New Testament, the idea that God stooped in Jesus can be found as a strong theological insight in other writers. Even though John's Gospel doesn't include the Nativity story as we know it, it does have the concept of the eternal *Logos* of God, the supreme rational principle of the universe, becoming flesh (1:14). Our word "logic" is related to *Logos* which indicates reason and rationality—the ultimate logic of the universe. It is usually translated into English as "Word". The idea that "the Word became flesh" contains the notion of God coming from eternity and taking flesh in the human life of Jesus. It is the focal point of the Prologue to John's Gospel (1:1–14) and certainly implies the idea of stooping, although this is not explained by the gospel writer himself. The word "incarnation" literally means an "embodiment" or "enfleshment" (from the Latin *incarnatus*) referring to the eternal God taking on human flesh.

This basic idea of God being embodied in Jesus was at the heart of centuries of debate in the Early Church as the so-called doctrine of the incarnation emerged. The many debates focused upon how humanity and divinity came together in the person of Jesus. The notion that Jesus was really human and really divine was based on the experience that God had been known in Jesus and that Jesus had shown human beings something new about God. The idea and experience of incarnation is connected to the idea and experience of God in creation. The thrust of this is that God is known through the material world, in nature and in human beings, and especially in Jesus. This carries with it the idea that God is positive about the material world, about creation and about bodies. It carries with it the idea that God affirms creation and sees it as basically good, as can be found in Genesis 1.

The notion of God stooping in the birth of Jesus is fundamental, then, to the picture of Jesus in the Gospels. It is the apostle Paul, however, who takes us further. Even though he seems to know nothing of the story of Jesus' birth in Bethlehem, he says a lot about God coming in Jesus in humility. Paul's letter to the Philippians is the key place where this comes out when he says that though Jesus was in the form of God he took the form of a slave and humbled himself. This passage in Philippians (2:6–11) is one of the most important in Paul's theology and in the New Testament as a whole. It is one of the so-called "Christological hymns" of the New Testament. It is a passage that has poetic structure and is finely balanced in the way it speaks of the significance of Jesus. He is "in the form of God" to begin with but is then humbled by becoming human and through the crucifixion. He does not hang onto his status as divine but becomes human and takes on the role of a slave.

The Greek word Paul uses here to say that Jesus "emptied himself" is *kenosis*. The claim is that in Jesus God "emptied himself" of his attributes as God and became human (v. 7). The overall pattern is clearly one of Jesus being with God, then "humbling himself" unto death, and finally being exalted to God's side once again. The word *kenosis* has given rise to the English word "kenotic", which is often used of this idea of God's self-emptying incarnation in Jesus. We can see here that the process of emptying is much the same as God "stooping" in Jesus.

This idea of God humbling himself can also be found in Paul's second letter to the Corinthians, a long and serious letter written to a community divided and in conflict over leadership and authority. Paul's words about Jesus are wrapped up in all manner of pastoral concerns and crises, but he is clear about who Jesus is and what he is like. In 8:9 Paul says that even though God was rich, he became poor in Jesus, so that Christians might become rich. Once again, this is in line with Paul's understanding that God came in humility in Jesus and is a humble God. This basic notion was one that was to remain central in later centuries: the incarnation was not only about God being in Jesus but about a humble God being shown in a humble life.

Conclusion

In this second week of Advent we have travelled in our imaginations to Bethlehem and the birthplace of Jesus. The Church of the Nativity, through its "door of humility" and the cave of Jesus' birth, has spoken to us of God "stooping" to come among us. We have seen that although the New Testament accounts of the birth of Jesus are very different from each other and from the version that comes to us in Nativity plays and Christmas carols there is, nevertheless, a common thread connecting the New Testament gospel accounts to the church in Bethlehem: Jesus' birth shows God coming to us in a humble form. Jesus is Emmanuel or "God with us". This idea of God humbling himself or stooping towards us in Jesus can also be found in the writings of the apostle Paul.

In Advent, as we consider the meaning of Jesus' birth and life today, it is important to remember that it was because of Jesus' life of humility and compassion that people saw God in a new light in him and remembered his birth and told stories about it. The notion of God dwelling in Jesus the "new temple" and the theology of humility in the door at the Church of the Nativity in Bethlehem both stand in line with the New Testament witness that God came in humility in this special birth. He stooped and came among us in Jesus, and it is to this specific presence in a person that we are called to respond in our Christian lives today.

Things to do

Bible study passages
- Matthew 1:18–25
- Luke 2:1–7
- Philippians 2:6–11

Worship
- Psalms: 98; 99; 139
- Hymns: Once in royal David's city; Meekness and majesty.

Activities
- Try squatting low or lying on the floor. How does your sense of space change?
- Look at some paintings, icons, mosaics or frescoes to see how God is portrayed spatially. For example, The Ancient of Days by William Blake or the well-known icon of the Trinity by Andrei Rublev.

Questions for discussion
- What are your feelings about marking the traditional place of Jesus' birth with a church?
- Why do you think there is so little in the New Testament about Jesus' birth?
- What do you understand by the idea that God "stooped" in the birth of Jesus?

Further reading
Trevor Dennis, *The Christmas Stories* (London: SPCK, 2007).

Edwin D. Freed, *The Stories of Jesus' Birth: A Critical Introduction* (Sheffield: Sheffield Academic Press, 2001).

Paula Gooder, *Journey to the Manger: Exploring the Birth of Jesus* (Norwich: Canterbury Press, 2015).

CHAPTER 3

Nazareth: Growing in Wisdom

The next part of our Advent journey takes us to Nazareth in Galilee where Jesus grew up. This very special town lies in the north of the Holy Land about an hour's drive west of the Sea of Galilee and about the same distance east of the Mediterranean. Nestling in the hills about 1,400 feet above sea level, it has spread over the centuries up the surrounding hillsides with the famous Jezreel Valley round about. A Palestinian Arab city inside Israel, Nazareth's inhabitants are Israeli Arabs. It has the greatest concentration of Palestinians inside Israel and is often known as the Palestinian capital of Galilee. In 1948, unlike Bethlehem, Nazareth was taken into Israel. Today, with a population of over 75,000, it is predominantly Muslim although the Christian presence is still strong. Nearby is the recently established modern Jewish community of about the same size known as "Nazareth Illit" or "Greater Nazareth".

In many respects, contemporary Nazareth feels much like Bethlehem. We arrive in a bustling Arab market town with centuries of history and tradition. Entering the Old City, we see shops and markets similar to those in Bethlehem and Jerusalem. Clothes stalls, food shops, religious souvenirs, coffee and baklava all abound. But at the time of Jesus, Nazareth was very much smaller than it is today. Most scholars estimate that only a few hundred people lived there. The first-century village was in the floor of the valley and was by all accounts something of a backwater. Today, it is a vibrant modern city with some of the worst traffic in the Holy Land! It remains a major attraction for modern Christian pilgrims.

Visiting Nazareth can be disorientating, until you get to know the place. It's a busy, modern city. But as we wander the streets in the centre of town, we become aware of its ancient levels and buildings, its importance to Christians and the sheer sense of life teaming forth all around us.

Walking the streets now, we get a sense of what it might have been like to grow up in Nazareth in the past. Watching children everywhere, playing on the pavements, on balconies of houses and in school yards, gives a real sense of life in this busy urban basin. Hearing the sounds of their voices echoing across the valley, we soon imagine the youthful Jesus in his home setting two thousand years ago.

In this chapter we shall think of Nazareth primarily as the place where Jesus grew up. It is our next lens for Advent, and one through which we can begin to imagine his historical location, what he believed and the life he must have led. Through this we can begin to think about his wisdom and his significance for our faith today. First, however, some general background.

What happened in Nazareth?

Like Jerusalem and Bethlehem, the name Nazareth conjures up all sorts of associations for Christians. The important things are: first, the annunciation or appearance of the angel Gabriel to Mary telling her that she would be the mother of Jesus (Luke 1:26–38); next, Jesus' childhood, adolescence and young adulthood about which we know next to nothing (Matthew 2:23; Luke 2:39–40); and finally, Jesus reading Isaiah 61 in the synagogue: "The Spirit of the Lord is upon me" (Luke 4:16–30). The second of these is our main interest here. But first, what do we know about Nazareth, and how does Jesus fit in?

Most of the Nazareth from Jesus' time is underneath and around the huge modern Roman Catholic Basilica of the Annunciation which dominates the city. Designed by the Italian architect Giovanni Muzio and completed in 1968, the huge black dome can be seen from just about everywhere in Nazareth. The church has two main levels, the lower one containing the "House of Mary" in which tradition maintains Mary received the message of the angel Gabriel at the annunciation. A cave is the focus over which different churches have been built through the centuries. Then, above, a huge church dominated by modern images of Mary and Jesus given by a variety of nations around the world. The

Basilica of the Annunciation stands on the site of previous churches in Nazareth.

As far as we can tell, there was no church in Nazareth in the fourth century: the pilgrim focus was on the birth, death and resurrection of Jesus in Bethlehem and Jerusalem. Nazareth was apparently relatively unknown: "Can anything good come out of Nazareth?" (John 1:46). However, by the sixth century there were churches commemorating the annunciation and the childhood of Jesus. In the eleventh century the Crusaders built an enormous cathedral which was destroyed in the twelfth century by Saladin at the famous Battle at the Horns of Hattin (1187). A small Franciscan chapel existed from the seventeenth century onwards but was destroyed in the 1960s to make way for the modern Basilica. The nearby Church of St Joseph is usually thought to mark the House of Joseph and of the Holy Family.

Generally, Nazareth is thought of as the location of Jesus' childhood and young adult life. Recent excavations in the area have revealed first-century houses and have made possible a real sense of what the town was like in the first century. It was here in this place that Jesus grew up and spent about thirty years of his life. Because we know hardly anything about these years, they are often called the "hidden years". The Gospels say next to nothing about them, but the Christian imagination has run wild filling in the detail! Apocryphal Gospels from the second century onwards have provided stories of Jesus playing as a child and of his activities at school.[12]

The New Testament Gospels have only two stories about Jesus' childhood. First, when he is taken to the Temple in Jerusalem by his parents for the purification (Luke 2:22–24). When they return to Nazareth, we are told: "The child grew and became strong, filled with wisdom; and the favour of God was upon him" (2:40). And second, when he travels to Jerusalem for the Passover at the age of twelve (2:41–52). After the celebration, when his parents begin the journey home, Jesus is left behind, only to be discovered three days later in the Jerusalem Temple "sitting among the teachers, listening to them and asking them questions" (2:46). After they return to Nazareth, we are told, "Jesus increased in wisdom and in years, and in divine and human favour" (2:52).

Nazareth is saturated with history and tradition. It is a place of stunning beauty to which pilgrims flock to remember the events of Jesus' early years. It is, of course, the town that has given Jesus part of his name: "Jesus of Nazareth". But it is Jesus' growth in wisdom in this location which forms our focus here. For although we know next to nothing about the major part of his life, Luke chooses to indicate twice that Jesus grew in wisdom in Nazareth. Another New Testament writer also uses this word of Jesus. What are we to understand by it?

How wise was Jesus?

What can we really know about the "hidden years" and about Jesus' growth as a child, teenager and adult? We appreciate more now than ever before that he was a first-century Jew of the period of the Second Temple in Jerusalem. From this we know that he would have believed in God the creator, in the Jewish covenant established at Sinai (the Decalogue or Ten Commandments) and in the authority of the Jewish Law or Torah (Genesis, Exodus, Leviticus, Numbers and Deuteronomy). He would obviously have followed the Jewish traditions and practices of his day. We know that he would have been circumcised on the eighth day after his birth and would have attended local synagogue gatherings in which young people learnt the Torah and the daily practices of their faith.

Although there was no Bible as such at the time, Jesus would have known authoritative writings such as the Psalms (often known as the "Prayer Book of the Second Temple"), the Prophets, the Books of Kings and the apocalyptic work Daniel. He would have learnt Hebrew and the dialect of Hebrew spoken in Galilee, the local Galilean Aramaic. It is also possible that he knew some Greek. He might also have travelled to nearby Sepphoris and experienced something of the Greek culture and learning in its theatre.

These basic facts about Jesus' early life and education would have been true of anyone growing up within the Judaism of the time. As for Jesus' particular profession, the Gospels use the Greek word *tektōn* (Mark 6:3) meaning "stonemason" as well as "carpenter", which broadens the traditional view somewhat. Beyond this it is difficult to know further detail or which of the many strands within Judaism Jesus belonged to. Judging broadly from the way he is portrayed in the Gospels, he was a radicalizer within his own faith rather than against the Judaism of his day. And it seems clear that he was not otherwise educated beyond the synagogue education of the time. The authority which he clearly has in the Gospels comes from God (e.g. Mark 1:22), and he is "teacher" or "rabbi" in a general sense rather than in the sense of any official training. Clearly, then, Jesus grew up and was educated within the general contemporary structures of his religion. Although not all scholars would agree, some have recently portrayed Jesus as a wisdom teacher or sage.[13]

Luke's comment that Jesus grew in wisdom can be taken in a general sense, but it also means something quite specific. By the time of Jesus, wisdom was already a very important concept in Judaism as well as in surrounding cultures and traditions. In Judaism it was associated in particular, of course, with King Solomon whose reputation for wisdom spread far and wide. The Queen of Sheba travelled to Jerusalem to meet Solomon and experience his wisdom for herself (1 Kings 10). The so-called Wisdom literature of the Old Testament (Job, Proverbs and Ecclesiastes) encapsulates some of this wisdom. The various books have their own emphases, but they all reflect on human experience, seeking answers to the many problems of life.

The Old Testament Book of Proverbs is a key work in the wisdom tradition and is full of pithy sayings summing up life in simple sentences.[14] At the heart of the wisdom tradition lies the desire to understand the meaning of life. It searches for the inner meaning and a deeper understanding of the way things are in the world. The sayings in Proverbs are the result of generations of experience, observation and discussion. And so we have sayings such as, "A soft answer turns away wrath, but a harsh word stirs up anger" (15:1) and, "The rich and the poor have this in common: the Lord is the maker of them all" (22:2). Such pithy sayings sum up eternal truths.

But in addition to this general sense of human wisdom, the Book of Proverbs personifies wisdom as a beautiful woman who plays an active part in God's creative purposes from the beginning. Proverbs 8 has wisdom calling out to people to pursue prudence and intelligence. The author says, "wisdom is better than jewels" (8:11). She was there with God at the beginning helping him create the world (vv. 22–31). Gradually, she came to be thought of as an element of God's inner personality. Wisdom herself says, "whoever finds me finds life" (v. 35), and the writer is clear that, "The fear of the Lord is the beginning of wisdom, and the knowledge of the Holy One is insight" (9:10). Clearly, wisdom lay at the heart of God's very nature and purposes and at the heart of faith in him. Ultimately, to know God and his ways was to be wise.

In view of this powerful sense within Judaism that wisdom was part of the way God deals with the world it is not surprising to find the early Christians using wisdom language about Jesus when they tried to describe who he was for them. Luke tells us nothing about what he means by Jesus "growing in wisdom", but the carefully chosen and deliberate word clearly associates Jesus with God and his purposes.

Before Luke wrote his Gospel, the apostle Paul had already used wisdom language of Jesus. In his first letter to the Corinthians written in the early 50s of the first century, Paul contrasts the wisdom of the world with the wisdom of God. The wisdom of the world was what we would think of as worldliness: knowledge, power and wealth. But Paul says that the wisdom of God is the opposite: ignorance, weakness and poverty. In the Greek tradition, philosophy was, of course, the "love of wisdom", and there were plenty of people who wanted to be wise in the sense of all-knowing. But Paul says that God's wisdom is more like ignorance. In fact, worldly wisdom is really foolishness and what looks foolish is God's wisdom. Paul says, "God chose what is foolish in the world to shame the wise" (1 Corinthians 1:27). His theology of foolishness and weakness runs throughout his letters, and he clearly sees Jesus as the perfect example of God's wisdom. Jesus' growth in wisdom means his growth in relation to God and God's ways with the world.

How you can be wise too

If God dwells in Jesus as a "new temple" and stoops to be in Jesus, and if Jesus shows us God's very nature through wisdom, what are the implications for contemporary Christians who wish to grow in wisdom during Advent? The word "wisdom" isn't used much these days, and we don't often hear people aspiring to be wise. In this section we look at some of the things that dominate our culture today and that people often think of as being "wise". But we shall see that God's wisdom is the opposite of these and can form the basis of a very different sort of life. Advent is a time to re-address what sort of life we might live as Christians.

In contemporary western societies, wisdom isn't usually thought of as something we need. If we think of wisdom at all, it's often in terms of knowledge or possessions. Worldly wisdom is accumulated knowledge and the things it can achieve. The recent "information explosion" is all about our acquisition and control of knowledge. In recent decades through developments in technology it has become possible, for example, to have such access to knowledge that we can answer any question at any time. Through the internet and the capacity of computers, iPads and smartphones we can now have any amount of knowledge at our fingertips at any moment. And it's not just knowledge in the sense of facts. We can have the entire works of William Shakespeare or of Beethoven in our pockets available at the click of an icon. If we think of wisdom at all, it probably means "knowing, experiencing or understanding a lot".

Wisdom is also often thought of as power and success. In contemporary western culture, the acquisition of wealth is often paramount in the minds of young people. Our society is competitive and geared towards winners. We think that happiness lies in power, wealth and possessions. People's understanding of their jobs and houses is often as status symbols. Their values are rooted in the things that money can buy. Their sense of achievement is focused on how far they have risen in their profession and in how much money they have made. We might add here the sense of physical strength and health as a type of wealth. To be ill or weak is often thought of as failure. In these senses, wisdom is thought of as possessions, wealth or strength and to be wise is to have done the right things.

In all this we can see Paul's "rulers of this age": knowledge, "human standards" or wealth and power (1 Corinthians 1–2). But Paul reminds us that this is worldly wisdom and that there is a different path: the way of Jesus Christ. His way is characterized by the opposites: ignorance, weakness and poverty. These are Paul's focal themes, and his message is crucial to Christian faith today. During Advent it is important to establish the sort of things that might help to create the possibility of a different sort of wisdom. I suggest these should include at least the following elements: listening, discernment, insight, humility and compassion.[15] Let us consider these in order.

First, listening. We live in a world full of chatter and noise. No one listens, even to the person speaking to them. The tendency is to talk constantly and exhaustingly. Dominance, strength, power and manipulation are the order of the day. People no longer stop to listen. But this would be the first act for a wise life today. Stop and listen to other people but also to creation, to music, to your own body. Listening, so familiar to musicians, will help you reconnect with your environment and context. Indeed, listening will enable you to hear new things or old things long forgotten.

This will then open the door to discernment or perceiving things at a different level, to appreciating something more than the surface babble of society and its concerns. Discernment will then lead to insight which is something that enables us to "see into" the meaning of things, something that takes us beyond the surface into the deeper meaning and value of things. The appreciation of value can then enable life to be lived at a different level of awareness.

This approach through listening establishes the possibility of different values and we can then find humility and compassion. There's no need to look further than Jesus of Nazareth to find the example of a humble life. Throughout the Gospels, he preaches, teaches and lives out a message of selflessness and humility. He is the one who tells his disciples to deny themselves and to put others first (Mark 8:34), who washes his disciples' feet and is the servant of all (Luke 22:24–27; John 13:1–20). And he is the one who is seen by others as embodying these values and acting them out even unto death. Paul, again, writes of Jesus becoming the servant of all and being exalted by God for it (Philippians 2:6–11). Indeed, this element of the "foolishness of God" lies at the heart of the theology of incarnation, of God's stooping towards the world in Jesus.[16]

Conclusion

At the end of this third week of Advent we have wandered the streets of Nazareth in our imaginations and got a feel for the place as it is today. We have seen something of the history of the town and imagined Jesus growing up there. We have followed Luke's lead that Jesus grew in wisdom in Nazareth, and we have thought a little bit about what that might mean for us today. We now have the following overall framework in mind: Just as God dwelt in the temple in Jerusalem, so he dwelt in Jesus of Nazareth. God stooped to dwell in Jesus not only in his birth but in his life. And the Jesus who grew up in Nazareth grew in wisdom, which means he grew in the likeness of the God who can be seen in him.

The wisdom of God spoken of by Paul is reflected in the wisdom of Jesus and can become the basis of our own wisdom and growth in Christian discipleship today.[17] If we are to grow in God's presence and be like God in wisdom, we must follow Jesus' path of humility and compassion for others. In this penultimate week of Advent, Nazareth has turned our hearts and minds to God's wisdom and to the task of growing in wisdom like Jesus, the one in whom God dwells. The final week for Advent focuses on our lives as baptized disciples.

Things to do

Bible study passages
- Proverbs 8:22–36
- Luke 2:39–40
- 1 Corinthians 1:18–31

Worship
- Psalms: 14; 37; 111
- Hymns: Immortal, invisible, God only wise; Lord of all hopefulness.

Activities
- Watch children playing and growing up in the area where you live. What do you notice about them?

- Ask some young people if they know what wisdom is.

Questions for discussion

- What do we learn about Nazareth from the New Testament?
- Why do you think Luke mentions Jesus "growing in wisdom"?
- Discuss ways in which Christians might grow in wisdom today.

Further reading

David J. Bryan, *Jesus: His Home, His Journey, His Challenge* (London: SPCK, 2013).

Rod Garner, *How to Be Wise: Growing in Discernment and Love* (London: SPCK, 2013).

Samuel Wells, *A Nazareth Manifesto: Being With God* (Oxford: Wiley, 2015).

CHAPTER 4

The River Jordan: Becoming a Disciple

We conclude the first part of this book at the River Jordan, the first moment of real decision. Christians all over the world know of the Jordan. It is the river in which Jesus was baptized by John the Baptist. The river itself is usually a surprise to visitors to the Holy Land. Most expect to see something like the Thames, Tiber or Mississippi but the Jordan is only a stream by comparison. Beginning in the north in Syria it is fed by the melting snows of Mount Hermon at Dan. There are two sections: the Upper Jordan (north of the Sea of Galilee) and the Lower Jordan (south of the sea). North of the sea, four smaller rivers run into the Jordan. South of the sea, it winds its way through the great Rift Valley or Jordan Valley below sea level all the way down to the Dead Sea where it evaporates. The name Jordan might originally have meant "coming down from Dan".

This very special winding river plays an important part in the Old Testament, is named in the Gospels and is famous in Christian hymns and songs such as, "On Jordan's bank, the Baptist's cry . . .", "Michael, row the boat ashore . . . (Jordan's river is deep and wide)" and many others. To this day it has a powerful symbolic place in the Christian imagination signifying formation, freedom, identity and healing. And because it's the river in which Jesus was baptized, it evokes all the significance of Christian baptism as well. In the Church's calendar Jesus' baptism is celebrated soon after Christmas in early January.

Getting to the River Jordan on the Holy Land side today is no straightforward matter. It runs through the Jordan Valley quite a way east of the main road and is mostly in a military zone. Imagine you are travelling through desert with dust blowing up all around you. You are in the region of Jericho about twelve hundred feet below sea level just north of the Dead Sea. You drive into an area with military security and then walk down to the river. The side you're on is the West Bank, and the other side is Jordan, the country. A number of modern churches have been built in this area in recent years, and it's become really popular with pilgrims. The water is often green, and there are trees and bushes all around. It's a good idea to get at least your feet wet. Some people go for total immersion! Getting into the water brings it alive and makes you feel very close to the events of scripture.

With such an important place in scripture and tradition, the River Jordan is ideal as our final Advent lens leading up to Christmas. Through it we look at Jesus' baptism and at our own commitment and discipleship. This then carries us into the second part of the book and forward into Lent.

Drawing the boundaries

Through most of history, the Jordan river has been a natural boundary. But it is also a symbolic boundary. Although the distance from the Sea of Galilee to the Dead Sea is only about sixty-five miles, the Jordan is about twice that length, because it constantly twists and turns. On average it is about a hundred feet wide, but can be much less. The importance of the river is, of course, that it is water. In recent years a number of factors have led to the river holding less water, including Israel giving water from the Sea of Galilee to the Hashemite Kingdom of Jordan on the other side of the river, and the many droughts that have affected the area. Pilgrims can visit the river at a number of places: one really commercialized and not far from the Sea of Galilee, and one already mentioned at the other end near Jericho which is now usually thought to be near the place where Jesus was baptized. It's also possible to visit the river in a number of other less well-known places.

The religious symbolism associated with the Jordan river appears early in the Old Testament. It concerns the formation of the people of Israel and their entry into the "promised land". The river is often mentioned as a boundary between some of the twelve tribes of ancient Israel, but more references concern Joshua leading the people of Israel from their desert wandering period across the Jordan into the land of Israel (Joshua 1–4).

Following their period in the desert, the people came up to the Jordan and crossed into the land of Canaan from the east. The Jordan Valley and the area near Jericho is desert land, stark and arid. Jericho is an oasis, but the area around it is dry and uninviting. In the Book of Joshua (3–4), the people pass through the Jordan on dry ground. Twelve stones symbolize the twelve tribes of Israel. The people cross carrying the Ark of the Covenant, containing the tablets of the Decalogue. The Ark was the symbol of God's presence among them. They cross the Jordan from one stage of their journey to another.

Crossing the river inevitably recalls the waters of creation in Genesis (1:1f) and the crossing of the Red Sea in Exodus (13:17–15:27). The Jordan symbolized freeing and establishing God's people and leading them into a new phase of their life. This time, it would be into a settled state of commitment to the God who had brought them up out of the desert and formed a covenant with them. From this time onwards, the Jordan river carried with it the symbolism of crossing a boundary and forming a new people, with a new phase of identity, commitment and responsibility. Because of the water, it resonated with the earlier Exodus experience and all its theological associations.

Jordan's symbolic power is also evident in the story of Naaman the Commander of the Syrian army (2 Kings 5). Naaman is high up in his country's military system and is a well-known figure in his community. He is successful and wealthy but he has found no healing for his leprosy through his own national Syrian god Rimmon. Naaman has heard of the prophet Elisha in Israel and decides he will seek his advice. When he gets to Israel, Elisha tells him to go and wash seven times in the River Jordan if he wishes to be healed. Naaman does this and is healed. The story shows that Yahweh the God of Israel is a God of healing and is also God of the whole world, not just of Israel. So now, in the time of Elisha, several centuries after the crossing into the Promised Land, the Jordan river still has significant power.

Already in the Old Testament, then, the River Jordan is a powerful symbol of formation, freedom, identity and healing. It is the place where the people of God are formed and given their identity. It is the place where they cross a boundary and begin their life as a new people. Not surprisingly, the river continues to carry these important associations after it has become the place of Jesus' baptism.

John baptizes Jesus

In the New Testament, Jesus is baptized in the River Jordan by John the Baptist. John himself is an important figure, and we hear about him in all four Gospels. He appears baptizing in the region of the Jordan river. We do not know exactly where, and, in any case, he probably moved about quite a bit. Christians often see John as the last of the Old Testament prophets or as the first of the New Testament figures to introduce Jesus.

John is certainly a desert figure with his camelhair suit and his diet of locusts and wild honey (Mark 1:6). Some think he was connected to the Essene community at Qumran either as a member or as an associate, but we cannot be certain. Probably poised against the Jerusalem Temple, the Essenes were strong in their belief that God was to act imminently to bring about the end of time. Whatever the truth about John's involvement with them, he knows the desert and clearly practised a water ritual like many of the Jews of his day.[18] He also preached a message of repentance and forgiveness introducing Jesus' own message of the kingdom of God (1:4).

It seems that John the Baptist had quite a following by the time he baptized Jesus and indeed Jesus may have been part of that. John probably came from a priestly family that was now turning against the temple authorities in Jerusalem. We know that John's father Zechariah worked as a priest in the temple as Luke begins his Gospel with Zechariah's vision in the temple and the birth of John (1:1–25 and 57–66). In fact, Luke tells us more about John than any other Gospel and spends quite a lot of time on the circumstances of John's birth. Later Christians identified a small village in the Judaean hills west of Jerusalem as John's birthplace. Since the early Byzantine period in the Holy Land the village of Ein Kerem has been associated with John's birth and with the visitation of Mary to Elizabeth. It is a beautiful location in which pilgrims still today reflect upon John's birth and significance.

However, it is clear in the Gospels that John only introduces Jesus. He is the precursor or announcer of Jesus. In the Orthodox Church John is known as the *prodromos* or forerunner of Jesus. In Mark's Gospel Jesus' ministry begins after John is arrested by Herod. The story of John's demise and death is well known: his head is chopped off at the request of Herod's daughter (Mark 6:14–29), an event which according to Josephus took place at Machaerus in present-day Jordan near the northern tip of the Dead Sea.[19] It is unfortunate that we don't know more about John, but once Jesus is baptized, he disappears, and Jesus becomes the focus of the gospel accounts.

It is unclear exactly where on the River Jordan Jesus was baptized and across the centuries several sites have been proposed. Matthew, Mark and Luke do not mention any specific location, but John's Gospel gives two. First, he says that John was baptizing "in Bethany across the Jordan" (1:28), presumably to distinguish it from the town of the same name near Jerusalem. But there is no evidence of a place called Bethany on the eastern side of the Jordan. There is an early manuscript of this Gospel which reads "Bethabara" instead of Bethany, and in the third century the Christian scholar Origen followed this reading. But no Bethabara has been found either! However, the Byzantine Christians built a church near the Jordan river in an area just north of the Dead Sea near Jericho (already mentioned at the beginning of this chapter) and thought this was the place. Recent excavations have uncovered foundations of a church, and the site has now become popular on both sides of the river. Pilgrims have started visiting this site in great numbers.

The Fourth Gospel also tells us that John the Baptist was baptizing "at Aenon near Salim" (3:23). However, this has been difficult to locate as well. In recent times the Israelis have opened a somewhat commercial place called "Yardenit" ("little Jordan"), which is a section of the river just south of the Sea of Galilee and to which thousands of Christians of many different types now flock for total immersion baptisms, renewal of baptismal vows and other ceremonies. Although the place has no claim to historical authenticity, it has become very popular. Of course, the Jordan can be visited at other places, particularly along the stretch of road north of the Sea of Galilee in the region closer to its sources at Mount Hermon.

The baptism of Jesus occurs in all four Gospels, although John's Gospel has only a passing reference (Matthew 3:13–17; Mark 1:9–11; Luke 3:21–22; John 1:32–34). In Mark it occurs at the beginning and is brief. Jesus comes up out of the water, the heavens are opened, and the Spirit comes upon him like a dove. Then, drawing on Psalm 2:7 a voice announces, "You are my Son, the Beloved; with you I am well pleased." It is clear that this event constitutes the beginning of Jesus' ministry. In the style of the prophetic calls of ancient Israel it establishes the beginning of the way things will be from now on. And Jesus is announced as God's Son. The account in Matthew is similar although there is the famous objection by John, but Jesus insists (3:13–17). Again, there is the Spirit and the voice. In Luke's version Jesus is at prayer following his baptism when the Spirit and the voice occur (3:21–22). But again, the significance and impact are the same.

Overall, Jesus' baptism marks the beginning of his ministry and inaugurates his role as Son of God. It also resonates with Israel's own story of crossing the Jordan boundary: a story marking formation, freedom, identity and healing. With Jesus' baptism at the River Jordan a new people is formed and the kingdom of God is launched.

What about your baptism?

The River Jordan and the baptism of Jesus invite us to reflect upon the meaning of our own baptisms. The practices of the many different churches vary when it comes to baptism, but there are basically two possible methods: we are either baptized as babies or as adults. We are either baptized with parents and godparents speaking on our behalf or as adults speaking for ourselves. For babies, the ceremony will be at a font and this is the procedure in the east and the west, although in the Orthodox Churches babies are baptized by total immersion usually with great excitement and pandemonium! In the west, babies are baptized by sprinkling on the forehead. In the Reformed Churches in the west, the baptism of adults is by total immersion. The theological differences are fundamental: for the young, the emphasis is on original sin: baptism washes away an inherited condition. For adults, the focus is on the response of the individual for herself.

Whichever way, the emphasis is on a new beginning and a new identity in which people are "born again" into the family of Christ. We are members by nature of the human family and of our particular family. In baptism we become members of the family or body of Christ. As at the Jordan, a boundary is crossed, a new identity is assumed and a new people is formed.

Advent is an appropriate time for us to reassess the meaning of our baptisms. In this season we focus on God coming to us. Baptism is one of those times when God comes to us in a particular way, and we respond in commitment and discipleship. In a special sense, baptism is the making of disciples, the making of Christians. It draws us into the family of Jesus and invites us to be different. It invites us to become like Jesus in the way we live and behave towards others and towards our environment. It invites us to take up the humility and compassion displayed by Jesus in his own life. It invites us to live the life of the kingdom of God as preached by Jesus, and it invites us to preach, teach and heal as he did.

In the thinking of all the churches, baptism is the fundamental action. It signifies the family of committed Christians, the common calling that we all share, to be drawn into the likeness of Jesus. There are different orders and roles within the churches but baptism is the basic state of all those in the family. There are numerous ways in which we can respond to our Christian calling and our attachment and association with our churches will enable us to grow in discipleship and increase our sense of faith and calling.

But it may not all be plain sailing. After his baptism, Jesus is driven by the Spirit into the desert to encounter the devil (Mark 1:12–13). Following his reception of the Spirit and announcement of his special place in God's purposes he is driven by the Spirit into a forty-days-long encounter with Satan! His temptations to turn stones into bread, to throw himself down from the temple and to worship Satan are all part of the challenge that confronts him not only in the desert but continuously. The life of the kingdom is for Jesus a constant struggle of encounter and temptation. We too must remember that life as baptized Christians will not necessarily mean that it will be easy. There will be challenges and difficulties to face and overcome, obstacles to get over and disappointments to carry. Our baptisms do not carry us into a life of ease and leisure.

Indeed, as the apostle Paul says in Romans 6, when we are baptized, we are baptized into Christ's death, we are buried with him, undergoing a death to our former selves and ways of life. Paul uses the language of death and burial to bring out the message that following Jesus, and being baptized into his family, means "dying" to the things of the past and to the things that we might otherwise have prioritized. This sense of going down into the grave with Christ is enacted especially in total immersion baptisms where the person's entire body goes under the water. Paul continues by reinforcing the connection: just as we are buried with Christ so shall we rise with him. As we come up through the water, we are raised with Christ. In other words, in being baptized we die and rise with Christ, taking part in his crucifixion and in his resurrection. As baptized Christians we "walk in newness of life" (6:4).

Conclusion

At the River Jordan a boundary has been crossed and a new people formed. Themes from Genesis, Exodus and Joshua have fed into the baptism of Jesus and reminded us of our own baptisms. We now see more clearly that Jesus' baptism and our own focus on formation, freedom, identity and healing. In this new family, people don't just "believe in God", they live a particular lifestyle based on Jesus' own life. Of course, it will not all be plain sailing. Temptations and challenges will continue. But our past lives of self-centredness have been left behind, our self-pursuit has gone, and the habit of always looking to our own needs first has died. Now we take on a new identity of humility and compassion in all things.

And so, during the four weeks of Advent we have considered some important aspects of Christian faith by looking through four lenses taken from the Holy Land. Jerusalem gave us "Jesus the new temple". Bethlehem gave us God "stooping" in Jesus. Nazareth gave us Jesus growing in wisdom and encouraged us to do the same. And finally, the River Jordan has reminded us of Jesus' baptism and our own. An important paradigm has emerged: God's presence in Jesus and our own response. The four chapters have provided us with some vivid images for thinking about Jesus and with some challenging issues that arise in following him. We are ready now, after a break, to embrace Lent.

Things to do

Bible study passages
- Joshua 3:1–17
- Matthew 3:13–17
- Romans 6:1–11

Worship
- Psalms: 74; 89; 93
- Hymns: On Jordan's bank, the Baptist's cry; Peace is flowing like a river.

Activities
- If there is a baptism anywhere in your area, try to attend.
- Go into a church and look at the font. What does it symbolize?

Questions for discussion
- What is the significance of water in the practice of baptism?
- How are we to understand the baptism of Jesus?
- Share your understanding of your own baptism.

Further reading
Ian Bradley, *Water: A Spiritual History* (London: Bloomsbury, 2012).
Timothy Radcliffe, *Take the Plunge: Living Baptism and Confirmation* (London: Bloomsbury, 2012).
Rowan Williams, *Being Christian: Baptism, Bible, Eucharist, Prayer* (London: SPCK, 2014).

Part Two: Lent to Easter

CHAPTER 5

The Desert: Resisting Temptation

In the first part of this book, the four weeks of Advent took us from Jerusalem through Bethlehem and Nazareth to the realm of decision-making at the River Jordan. Now, in Lent, through a further set of Holy Land lenses, we probe even more deeply into our sense of God's presence in our lives and our responses as disciples of Jesus.

Lent begins in the desert, and the Holy Land is mostly desert apart from the lush parts around the Sea of Galilee. Even Jerusalem is a city in the desert, although these days it is very built up and westernized. Deserts vary: some are flat like the Gobi or the Sahara. Others are rocky and hilly like the deserts of the Holy Land. The defining factor is rainfall. Most deserts have only a few inches of rain a year, and that's what makes them dry and barren. Deserts seem to lack the things we take for granted such as flora and fauna. They seem "deserted", silent and empty. And, of course, there's no water—until you find an oasis. The desert takes you out of your "comfort zone" making you feel exposed, threatened and lost.

At the beginning of Lent our first lens from the Holy Land is the desert, and the Judaean Desert in particular. Imagine Jesus being driven into the desert by the Spirit to be tempted by the devil. Our English versions of the Gospels usually say Jesus was driven into the "wilderness", conjuring up images of overgrown foliage and entangled trees. But the wilderness of the Gospels is the local desert around Jerusalem: the Judaean Desert. The Greek word is *eremos*, referring to the relatively barren, hilly and sandy area to the east and south of Jerusalem. It continues south to the west of the Dead Sea and turns into the Negev Desert around Beersheba. This continues all the way south to Eilat on the Red Sea. Further south still is the Sinai Desert of Egypt.

It's a very good idea if possible to spend some time in a real desert. The experience stays with you for life and can be a real shift in perception, not just of the physical but also of the spiritual. If you can't get to a real desert, imagine one. The Judaean Desert is mountainous and rocky. Everything looks brown and barren. Imagine you're dropping down by road from 2,500 feet above sea level to about 1,200 feet below, the lowest point on earth.

Your ears pop on the way! Communities of Bedouin can be seen by the roadside, and soon the great ships of the desert, the camels, appear moving slowly along. It's a change of landscape and a reorientation of the senses. As you get further down, you feel a long way from the comforts you're used to. You're gradually being immersed in a new environment. Imagine you're camping in the desert, so you see it by night and in the early morning. You see the changes of light and the wild animals. You then walk out with a trained guide and spend some time in solitude. As the place soaks into you, you slowly appreciate its silence and stillness, and a change of awareness gradually comes over you.

Desert spirituality

In the fourth century, Christian monasticism developed and flourished in the deserts of the Holy Land.[20] The desert fathers and mothers took off to the barren places around Jerusalem convinced that a deeper experience of God awaited them there. They went in search of solitude and silence and to separate themselves from the many distractions of city life. Desert monasticism began in Egypt and grew quickly in Judaea, Gaza, Syria and Asia Minor or what is now Turkey.

The beginnings of the search for God in the desert are usually traced to Antony of Egypt in the third century. We know about his life from the biography written by the great Athanasius with whom he was associated.[21] Antony sought solitude in the deserts of Lower Egypt and soon attracted disciples and wrote a Rule. His life was characterized by prayer, spiritual discipline and the battle with evil. Others in Egypt were Paul of Thebes and Pachomius.

The retreat to the desert can also be seen through the writings of later monks such as the famous John Climacus, Abbot of St Catherine's

Monastery at Sinai, and Chariton, Euthymius and Theodosius in Judaea. In Gaza there were Hilarion, Isaiah and Barsanuphius. And there were also women who formed monastic communities. Melania, for example, had a monastery on the Mount of Olives in Jerusalem. Then there were those in Syria, perhaps more eccentric, such as Simeon the Stylite, who lived on top of a pillar, and those in Cappadocia under Basil of Caesarea who also wrote a Rule. These figures were central to the development of monasticism and ultimately influenced western monasticism such as the Benedictines and the Franciscans whose rules and ways of life are rooted in theirs.

When these fathers and mothers retreated to the desert, they were seeking God in solitude and silence. They withdrew from city life and the responsibilities of work and family. They withdrew seeking a different experience in the unique stillness of the desert. The desert monastic tradition developed into two main types: the eremitic and the coenobitic. The eremitic (from the Greek *eremos*: desert) was essentially the hermit type. They lived alone with very little contact with others. The second type, the coenobitic (from the Greek *koinonia*: fellowship) were like the monasteries we know today. Sometimes there was a mix of the two types as in the Lavras of Egypt.[22] The monks would spend most of the time alone but meet once or twice a week for the Eucharist. And the hermit types were usually under obedience to an appointed leader.

The monastic life of the desert focused on training the body, mind and soul in the service of God. Indeed, the desert monks are often called "spiritual athletes", for it was a life of physical training designed to enable the soul to grow closer to God. In addition to solitude and silence they lived lives of obedience and prayer. They were celibate and ate and slept little. In prayer and contemplation they focused on repentance and self-examination, seeking greater self-knowledge, purity of heart and motivation. They learnt through a strict lifestyle to control their passions and fight off the many temptations, which they interpreted as demons. The temptations included fornication, anger, pride and gluttony. Above all, the monks trained in humility, putting others first and denying the self.

The ascetic life of the desert was balanced by manual labour in growing food, cooking, baking and weaving baskets. The roots of the later combination of prayer and manual work in the Benedictine tradition can be seen here. The desert monks had given up ordinary life with its support of family and friends. They had withdrawn from society, giving up their possessions and wealth. They had embraced poverty and simplicity and had made a significant break with the past in their search for a new experience of God. The call of the desert was strong and the experience challenging and formative. A great deal can still be learnt today from the desert and its monastic traditions.

The temptations of Jesus

Lent marks the forty days Jesus spent in the desert being tempted by the devil. His "temptations" are an important stage in the development of his identity. It is significant that Jesus' time in the desert (related in all three synoptic Gospels: Matthew 4:1–11, Mark 1:12–13 and Luke 4:1–13, though not in John) follows his baptism in the River Jordan by John the Baptist. At his baptism Jesus is announced by the voice of God to be "Son of God". Now, in the temptations, his sonship is tested. The simplest account is in Mark where we are told only that the Spirit drove Jesus into the desert for forty days, where he was tempted by the devil with the wild beasts and the angels ministered to him. It is important that it is the same Spirit that comes upon Jesus at his baptism that then also drives him into the desert to face the devil.

In Matthew and Luke there are additional details which make Jesus' encounter with the devil much more dramatic. It is these texts that include the "temptations" by the devil. There are three in each account. In Matthew we have the devil tempting Jesus to turn stones into bread, to jump down from a pinnacle of the Jerusalem Temple, and to bow down and worship the devil and receive all the kingdoms of the world. Included in the encounter are Jesus' quotations from the Book of Deuteronomy and the devil's replies. In Luke the encounter is essentially the same, but the order of the second and third temptations in Matthew is inverted.

In both accounts, we have a confrontation with evil: the possibility of miraculous and spectacular demonstrations of Jesus' status before God, the possibility of owning worldly kingdoms, and the possibility of worshipping the devil. In each case, through demonstrating his knowledge of the God of scripture and his own personal relationship with God, Jesus stands his ground and stays on God's side. It is not that Jesus is incapable of being tempted. His humanity surely includes this possibility. But it is his ability to withstand temptation that comes over strongly in the accounts. And this is why the angels minister to him (Matthew 4:11).

Jesus' temptations are fundamentally related to his baptism. At his baptism he receives the Spirit. At his temptations he rejects the devil. And in one sense after the temptations he is ready to begin preaching the kingdom of God (Mark 1:15). But the temptations are not a once-for-all encounter with evil which needs no further attention. In fact, the Spirit drives him into a continuous confrontation with the devil, as can be seen from the many subsequent occasions in the Gospels when Jesus is involved with exorcisms and other encounters with evil (e.g. 1:21–28; 5:1–20). The kingdom of God is continually in confrontation with evil and the struggle is a permanent part of Jesus' ministry in overcoming death.

Jesus' retreat to the desert already has a strong background in the Old Testament. The faith of ancient Israel emerged in the desert, and the desert plays a key part in the narratives about major figures. The great leaders and prophets of ancient Israel are people of the desert. The stories of Abraham in Genesis are all set in the desert terrain. He sets out in faith from Ur of the Chaldees and travels through desert to the Negev (Genesis 12:1–9). His faith is born in the desert.[23] The accounts of Moses at the Burning Bush (Exodus 3:1–6) and at Mount Sinai with the giving of the Ten Commandments, the establishment of the Covenant and the forty years of wandering (Exodus 33–34) take place in the desert of Sinai. The arrival of the children of Israel in the Promised Land is then focused in the Negev and Judaean deserts (Joshua 3–4).

Later, the prophet Elijah travels through the deserts of the region down to Sinai or Horeb, where he encounters God not in the earthquake or in the wind and fire but in "a sound of sheer silence" (1 Kings 19:12). It is the silence of God in the desert that affects Elijah most. Obviously the natural setting in these stories is the desert, but it is significant that the encounters are set away from cities and towns. In the Judaism of the time of Jesus a community known as the Essenes withdrew to the Dead Sea area at Qumran and lived a life of strict discipline seeking God. In the New Testament, John the Baptist appears baptizing in the Jordan Valley

(Mark 1:4). In all this, God is encountered in desert places. And those who experience him most deeply do so in the desert.

The fathers and mothers of the desert in the fourth century and afterwards saw themselves as standing in the footsteps of Abraham, Moses, Elijah and John. They saw their retreat to the desert as thoroughly biblical. Not least, they saw themselves as standing in line with Jesus himself. Their desert experience was rooted in Jesus' own encounter with the devil. And as they embraced a simple life and encountered God in the desert they recalled Jesus' own encounter with the devil. Jesus' own temptations and the way he responded provided a model for the later "athletes" of the desert.

During Lent, our minds are focused on the desert and on the temptations of Jesus. They can help provide a model for us as we attempt to live a truly Christian life in the modern world, albeit in very different circumstances. The desert has a great deal to teach us about resisting temptation and about simplicity of life. It can play an important part in helping us reconsider the real direction of our lives. And all of this will help us, as it did Jesus, in embracing the kingdom of God. In Lent we must ask ourselves in what ways we can "resist temptation" and grow in awareness of God.

Tempting and testing

So what are the messages of the desert and the temptations of Jesus for us as we begin Lent? Many of the things we usually associate with Lent have a long tradition: fasting, simplicity of life, good works and detachment from possessions. But these things mostly need to be re-imagined and re-claimed in a culture that is largely stacked against them today. For a start, there are messages of faith and commitment from the story of Abraham. He is no perfect pioneer of faith but an ordinary man who is able to leave things behind and set off on a new path in spite of his weaknesses and limitations. Lent provides us all with the chance to ask ourselves once again, "what does our faith mean to us?" and "Can we leave behind all those things that prop us up?" "Can we re-focus ourselves in the direction of God instead of seeking and serving ourselves all the time?"

And then there is Elijah whose desert encounter with God was not in the drama of wind, earthquake or fire but in the "sound of sheer silence". Our Lenten journey needs to include time in solitude and silence. This will start to change our perception of the world and of other people. We can be regenerated and re-energized by God's silence and re-oriented in a Godly direction. This can be done by establishing a rhythm of silence at home and through Quiet Days and retreats. The fathers and mothers of the desert also teach us some strong lessons about Lent. It is an opportunity for solitude and silence, for self-examination and re-assessment, for spiritual athletics, and a little withdrawal from self-satisfaction and complacency.

But the most important thing, the overarching element of our Lenten challenge, comes from Jesus' temptations in the desert. His encounter with the devil brings him into a decisive confrontation, which is more a matter of testing and orientation than anything else. It is a question of which way his life will go, what will concern and occupy him, and which overall direction his life will take. This is the fundamental question that Jesus faced and one that faces Christians at all times but especially in Lent. What do we really want? What do we really care about? And who do we really follow? Where are we ultimately oriented? These are questions that we should live with all the time, but Lent is an opportunity to face them again and try to refocus our answers.

In Jesus' temptations he is faced with the possibility of producing food in the midst of his desert fast. "Command these stones to become loaves of bread" (Matthew 4:3; cf. Luke 4:3), says the devil. It is a temptation to do something miraculous to solve the problem of hunger but also poses the question of what place food has in the general scheme of things. Jesus replies that we cannot live on bread alone and that we need God as well. The place of food and of hunger is in the forefront here. In our country most people have enough to eat, and many in the western world have too much. It is not widely appreciated that it is not always appropriate to eat unlimited amounts of food. Fasting and abstinence are not widely valued as a virtue in our culture but in Lent we learn that it is better to be in control of our eating than have it control us. In other words: are we oriented simply towards self-satisfaction and self-gratification or can we put that in context and realize that it is not the only thing in our God-given lives?

The next part of the narratives concerns the temptations to satisfaction, power and possession. The devil takes Jesus to the pinnacle of the temple asking him to throw himself down. This is the temptation to power and success, to spectacular feats and worldly glory. We are all caught up in this kind of temptation to worldly success. In a culture driven by competition and celebrity status we are all caught up in a process that often feels like education and progress: to achieve more and more is to be more successful and more fulfilled. We are often in the grip of this type of dynamic without even knowing it. But the celebrity culture that breeds the desire for more and more public success can often be destructive and corrosive of real long-lasting values.

The third temptation of Jesus is to possess the kingdoms of the world. This is perhaps the ultimate temptation, to power. Again, our culture is caught up in the drive towards possessions, of material things and of status. Usually it is a matter of money and financial gain that gets a grip on us and becomes our ultimate value.[24] The temptations of Jesus challenge all these things and confront us with what we really care about. "Where your treasure is," Jesus says later on, "there your heart will be also" (Matthew 6:21).

Conclusion

At the beginning of Lent, the deserts of the Holy Land and the temptations of Jesus help us re-orient ourselves towards God. The Judaean Desert around Jerusalem is the one associated with Jesus' temptations and the contemporary monasteries in that area bear witness to the long tradition of withdrawal to the desert. The desert enables a change of awareness and a new appreciation of God.

The physical deserts of the Holy Land connect with the spiritual deserts of our lives. Just as Jesus withdrew into the desert at the beginning of his ministry, and the desert fathers and mothers withdrew into the physical desert, so during Lent we can withdraw into our spiritual deserts, for solitude, silence and self-examination. Here in the silence we can be stripped bare of temptations to wealth, worldly possessions, power and control, and move more seriously into the presence of God and into the experience of Jesus in whom he dwells. Here in the desert experience as we struggle with demons and temptations, we too can find a new experience of the God Jesus knew and begin to gauge our responses to him.

Things to do

Bible study passages
- Genesis 12:1–9
- 1 Kings 19:1–18
- Luke 4:1–13

Worship
- Psalms: 23; 46; 77
- Hymns: Forty days and forty nights; Lead us, heavenly father, lead us.

Activities
- Make a list of the things that tempt and distract you.
- Try to spend some time in a real desert or a place of solitude and contemplation.

Questions for discussion
- What is the meaning of the temptations of Jesus?
- Discuss any contemporary "temptations" that might distract from living a Christian life.
- How important is silence to Christian life and prayer?

Further reading
Beldon G. Lane, *The Solace of Fierce Landscapes: Exploring Desert and Mountain Spirituality* (Oxford: Oxford University Press, 1998).
Alexander Ryrie, *The Desert Movement: Fresh Perspectives on the Spirituality of the Desert* (Norwich: Canterbury Press, 2011).
Meg Warner, *Abraham: A Journey Through Lent* (London: SPCK, 2015).

CHAPTER 6

Galilee: The Kingdom of God

From a boat on the Sea of Galilee you can see many of the places associated with Jesus' ministry in the Gospels. The Holy Land is small, and the area around the Sea of Galilee is very small. Pilgrims to the area love to get out onto the water to experience the silence and peace and get an overall perspective. Imagine we're boarding a medium-sized tourist boat to go out into the middle of the lake. We move off slowly onto the water, getting oriented to the skyline with a map and guide book.

But as we set off, the sense of the lake overtakes us. A haze of heat hangs over the water and things flicker in and out of sight. After twenty minutes or so, the driver suddenly switches off the engine and lets the boat float silently near the centre of the lake. It's a sublime experience. The silence isn't just tangible: it's staggering. Most of us have never experienced anything like this before. We wait and savour the moment, with a deep sense of stillness and inner calm, appreciating the vision Jesus of Nazareth had in this region.

When the engine re-starts we get our bearings again and start picking out a few places around the lake. This is the geographical setting of Jesus' ministry, and we soon get a real sense of the context and location of his work. This is the setting of many of the gospel stories. From the boat we can see pretty well the entire coastline around, and there's a feeling that at least on the eastern side nothing much has changed since Jesus' time. Suddenly, the picture of a Galilean rabbi from Nazareth operating in the small villages around the lake gets clearer. Somehow, he is with us through historical and geographical imagination.

The Sea of Galilee is actually a freshwater lake connected to the River Jordan north and south. At about seventeen miles long, thirteen miles wide and thirty-two miles around, it is the main body of water in the country and lies over 600 feet below sea level. In mood and ethos it's not unlike one of the lakes of the English Lake District, and at different times of day and year it can have very different moods, light and weather. It also has several different names: the Sea of Galilee, the Sea of Tiberias and Lake Kinneret. And it contains a wide variety of fish. The famous storms we know from the Gospels arise quickly through wind hurtling down surrounding valleys and hitting the water when it's raining.

The area around the Sea of Galilee is our next Lenten lens. Through it we will see something of Jesus' "Galilean vision" of the kingdom of God and once again glimpse aspects of the presence of God in his life.[25]

The Galilean vision

Looking north from the lake you're looking into the Upper Galilee. Looking south, down towards the West Bank. Looking east is the Hashemite Kingdom of Jordan, and west are the mountains of Israel in the direction of Nazareth and the Mediterranean Sea. At the time of Jesus the coastline of the lake was populated with small villages whose inhabitants made their living from fishing and agriculture. A few years ago when the lake was low in a drought some of the ancient harbours were revealed, and a first-century boat was discovered in the sea bed at Kibbutz Ginosar, where it is now on permanent display.

Among the places of Jesus' ministry, you will soon spot Capernaum, his headquarters after leaving Nazareth. Mentioned frequently in the Gospels, it takes its name from someone called Nahum, although we don't know who he was. Originally a small fishing village, it is no longer inhabited. The remains include an ancient synagogue dating from well after the time of Jesus as well as a possible house church that grew to be a Byzantine-period Christian pilgrim church. More recently a modern church has been built on the site with a glass floor through which you can see some of the ancient remains. Most striking, perhaps, are the remains of the first-century streets and houses, giving an excellent sense of what the town was like in Jesus' day. Here in Capernaum he cast out an unclean spirit in the synagogue (Mark 1:21–28) and healed a paralytic in a nearby house (2:1–12).

Also visible from the lake is Mount Beatitudes and the Church of the Beatitudes designed by the Italian architect Antonio Barluzzi. This wonderful little church is visible from miles around and has become a well-known landmark in the area. It is a black and white octagonal church built in 1938 and is based on the eight beatitudes from the Sermon on the Mount in Matthew 5–7. The church stands in beautiful grounds with exquisite gardens suitable for prayer, meditation and reflection. From the church balcony and gardens there are stunning views of the surrounding area.

Another important place is Tabgha, associated with Jesus' feeding of the five thousand (Mark 6:35–44). This has two churches: a Byzantine-style building completed in 1982 which belongs to the German Roman Catholic Benedictines. There were previous churches on the site, and it has been a place of prayer since the fourth century. Then, a glorious little church on the edge of the lake (sometimes the water is lapping close to the entrance) known as Peter's Primacy and recalling Jesus' words to Peter, "You are Peter, and on this rock I will build my church . . . " (Matthew 16:18) as well as Jesus' question to Peter, "Do you love me?" (John 21:15–19).

Not far away, out of sight from the lake, are other places known to us from the Gospels: Bethsaida, the home of some of the disciples (John 1:44); Chorazin, mentioned with Bethsaida and Capernaum as a place that needed to repent (Matthew 11.21–24). And at the other end of the lake, Kursi, commemorating the healing of the man known as Legion because he possessed many demons: the Gerasene demoniac (Mark 5:1–20). This has also been a place of prayer since the early days of Christianity and had the biggest monastery in the Holy Land in the Byzantine period. Across the other side of the lake, Tiberias, now a modern Israeli holiday centre, sprawls up the hillside.

Together, these places around the lake form the context of Jesus' ministry in the Gospels. Most of them have been places of prayer and pilgrimage for sixteen hundred years, and they all play a powerful part in stimulating the imaginations of Christian pilgrims who visit them today. For those looking for the historical Jesus, Galilee is exciting and challenging. For those seeking the Christ of faith it is inspirational. The Sea of Galilee and its surrounding villages were the setting of Jesus' ministry and inspired his vision of the kingdom of God. What exactly was his message?

Teaching, preaching and healing

The area around the Sea of Galilee is a good place to focus on the teaching of Jesus.[26] It is so moving that it is difficult not to imagine him there *in situ*. And in imagining him in his own historical setting a number of questions immediately arise: "What was he really all about?", "What did he stand for?", "What were his values?" and "What did he live and die for?" In Nazareth during Advent we got a sense of the context in which Jesus grew up. Now, in the places associated with him around the lake we can glimpse something of what he was about through his basic teaching on the kingdom of God.

One of the best ways of imagining Jesus is as a "teacher, preacher and healer", and these are all inter-related. Obviously there are many things that can be said about who he was both in terms of history and in terms of his divinity. Recent scholars have debated whether Jesus is best seen as a prophet, a sage, a magician or a stoic. Others see him more in terms of his specific relationship with God or his divinity. The various titles used about him in the New Testament such as "Son of God", "Son of Man", "Christ", "Lord", "Word" and "Wisdom" are all ways of thinking of him. But as we imagine him simply as the rabbi or teacher from Nazareth, ministering in the villages around the Sea of Galilee, the focus on teaching, preaching and healing provides a vivid picture.

It is clear from the Gospels that Jesus was a teacher. The word rabbi, used of him in the Gospels, means simply "teacher". Jesus isn't someone with training in teaching, however, but someone whose authority is so striking that it seems to come straight from God (Mark 1:22). Jesus teaches in synagogue gatherings as well as out in the open. And a great deal of the gospel narratives concern his teaching. He teaches in both word and deed, in the style of the prophets of ancient Israel. Imagining Jesus as a prophet adds to the picture of him as a teacher. He stands up and speaks out in public as well as demonstrating his teaching through the things he does. A good deal of Jesus' teaching comes to us in the Gospels as parables and these capture his basic vision of the kingdom of God.

A "parable" is basically a "comparison" or an analogy. Usually a story or an illustration, it trades on a point of similarity. Parables can be short sayings, longer narratives, pithy one-liners or longer comparisons. Some parables are allegories with several points. The process by which the parables got into the Gospels is complex, and we cannot always say that the form of a parable we now have comes directly from Jesus himself. But many of them are likely to have come from him. So, the parables of Mark's Gospel such as the Parable of the Sower, the Parable of the Mustard Seed and the Parable of the Seed Growing Secretly are likely to go back to Jesus himself (Mark 4:1–34).

Some of the other well-known parables in the Gospels are from Luke, such as the Good Samaritan (Luke 10:25–37), the Lost Coin (15:8–10) and the Prodigal Son (15:11–32). Others are in both Luke and Matthew, such as the Lost Sheep (Matthew 18:12–14; Luke 15:3–7). Others are in Matthew alone, such as the sheep and goats (Matthew 25:31–46). In John's Gospel things are somewhat different, and there are no parables in the style of the synoptics. Rather, Jesus' teaching is in long drawn-out discourses attached to the important signs revealing who he is (e.g. 6:1–71).

And throughout the Gospels, Jesus' teaching is also in deed and action. He doesn't just teach a message or a view of life. He isn't just a philosopher or even a wisdom teacher. He also gets down to the practical business of practising what he preaches, combining preaching and healing with his teaching. He demonstrates his message of the kingdom through healing the sick (Mark 2:1–12), casting out demons (Matthew 8:28–34), raising the dead (Luke 7:11–17) and calming a storm on the Sea of Galilee (Mark 4:35–41). His teaching, preaching and healing are all inter-related and form part and parcel of his whole purpose.

And all this is based on Jesus' basic vision of the "kingdom of God" or "kingdom of heaven". The first thing he announces in Mark's Gospel is: "The time is fulfilled, and the kingdom of God has come near; repent, and believe in the good news" (1:15; cf. Matthew 4:17). There is no doubt that this is Jesus' central message, what he lived and died for. The question of what the kingdom actually is, of course, has been discussed at great length by scholars for centuries, and there have been many different shades of opinion. But it remains Jesus' most important message and he taught his followers (in "The Lord's Prayer") to pray for its coming: "Your kingdom come" (Matthew 6:9–13; Luke 11:2–4).[27]

The kingdom of God is clearly the "reign" or "rule" of God. Jesus believed in the creator God of Israel, the one who had created the world and called together a people. In the Old Testament it is in the Psalms and the prophetic writings that we hear most about God being a king and having a kingdom (Psalm 99:1; Isaiah 6:5). Now in his own day Jesus was announcing a new phase in God's purposes which he probably saw himself as inaugurating. It is clear that Jesus did not think of the kingdom of God as lying in the future or in the other world. Nor did he see it as an individual, personal or spiritual thing. He saw the kingdom as God's rule for the whole of creation bringing about a new age in which all people would be included. Jesus' teaching, preaching and healing concerned a physical, tangible this-worldly reality affecting everyone. It was communal rather than individual and social rather than narrowly political. But it concerned life as it is actually lived, communities as they relate to each other and societies as they treat each other. As far as Jesus was concerned, the kingdom of God was a this-worldly, rather than an other-worldly, reality. So what are its defining features?

The Sermon on the Mount

The "Galilean vision" of Jesus focused on his message of God's kingdom or rule. What can we take away from this vision for our own Christian lives this Lent? Probably the most challenging part of Jesus' Galilean teaching is the Sermon on the Mount (Matthew 5–7; compare Luke's Sermon on the Plain, 6:17–49).[28] In Matthew the symbolism of the mountain presents Jesus as a new Moses. Just as Moses went up the mountain to commune with God and receive the Law (Exodus 19–20), so Jesus gives a "new law" from a mountain. Like Moses, Jesus provides a "new law" for his followers.

The Sermon on the Mount has often been called a "manual of Christian discipleship". It is a guide for Christian living. It's the handbook that goes with the job that needs doing and has seriously practical dimensions. It's often been thought of as the essence of Christianity, what it all "boils down" to. The only problem is that it isn't easy. The ethics of the Sermon on the Mount have often been called "an impossible ideal" and something unachievable. But it lies at the heart of Jesus' message of the kingdom and contains the ideals for which he lived and died.

In reality, there probably wasn't a single sermon or occasion when Jesus delivered all the teaching we now have in Matthew 5–7. Some scholars even question whether it all goes back to Jesus. But in any case it seems to sum up the heart of his message. It has to do with practical Christian religion, not "beliefs" so much as how you live your life on a day-to-day basis. It has to do with integrity, genuineness of faith and practice.

The first part of the sermon is the so-called Beatitudes, a series of eight sentences that begin "Blessed" and which are commemorated in Barluzzi's octagonal church by the Sea of Galilee (Matthew 5:3–12). In the Bible, different Hebrew and Greek words lie behind our English words "blessed" and "happy" and have a wide range of different meanings. The main idea, however, is that those who are "blessed" by God are those who are in a right relationship with him. To be "blessed" means to be on the right side of God, to know his favour, goodness and peace. To be "blessed" is the opposite of being "cursed".

Here in Matthew 5 those who are "blessed" are people whose spirit is weak and who mourn, the meek, the hungry and thirsty, the merciful, the pure, the peacemakers, and those who are persecuted. These are the people who know what God is really like. These people are salt and light for the world. And here we also have the exhortation to excel in righteousness (vv. 13–20). Much of this is typical of the type of "turn-the-world-upside-down" values of the kingdom of God that Jesus preaches in his parables.

The next section includes the so-called "antitheses": "You have heard that it was said . . . But I say to you . . . " (vv. 21–48). The Jewish Law is radicalized and tightened here, not replaced. People already know, for example, not to kill or not to commit adultery, but they are asked here not even to get angry or look lustfully at someone. In the kingdom, the standard is higher and Christians are required not even to think of revenge. Here also are the commands to "turn the other cheek", give another garment when someone wants your coat, and go the extra mile. The command isn't just to "love your neighbour" but also to "love your enemies". This ultimate challenge still shocks the most committed

Christians today. By the end of Matthew 5 we are commanded to, "Be perfect, therefore, as your heavenly Father is perfect" (v. 48). It is a tall order, demanding nothing less than everything.

Matthew 6 focuses on the practice of religion, not showing off in public, avoiding hypocrisy and false piety. These things bring their own reward. Jesus gives the Lord's Prayer in this chapter along with the line that sums us all up: "Where your treasure is, there your heart will be also" (v. 21). Ultimately, we are followers of the things that rule our hearts. Christians cannot serve two masters (God and money, see v. 24) but must decide between them. And so we are exhorted not to be anxious about selfish needs, even basics which keep us alive, for God will look after us (vv. 25–34).

The final chapter of the sermon calls for a non-judgemental life culminating in the so-called "Golden Rule": "In everything do to others as you would have them do to you . . . " (7:12). The life disciples are asked to lead is demanding; the gate is narrow. It is a life free of falsity and double standards. We will get out what we put in and are encouraged to take a look at ourselves rather than be critical of others. The good tree bears good fruit and the bad tree bad fruit. It's not just about doing things in God's name but about getting our hearts in order and putting ourselves last. The chapter culminates with a parable inviting us to consider what our faith is based upon: two men build houses, one on rock, the other on sand. When the wind and rain come, the house built on rock stands firm while the other collapses (vv. 24–27). It is the same with faith: it must be built on the values that have been outlined in the sermon. These are the guidelines for those who would be disciples of Jesus. This is his Galilean vision of the kingdom of God.

Conclusion

In this second week of Lent our lens has been the area around the Sea of Galilee. We have thought of Jesus as a teacher, preacher and healer and have looked briefly at his message of the kingdom of God. And we have focused on the Sermon on the Mount with its powerful message of service to others, even our enemies. The Galilee lens has been a vivid and colourful perspective through which to see what Jesus was all about. We have glimpsed the presence of God in him, in his vision of the kingdom and in his way of living that out. The challenge now is for us to embrace his message as disciples and followers.

How much of that message can we hold before us as something that might re-order our lives and change the world today? How much of the "handbook of Christian discipleship" are we willing and able to make our own? And how much of the Sermon on the Mount can we honestly say we take seriously on a regular basis? Lent provides an opportunity for us to ask ourselves these questions afresh and to make some decisions for the future.

Things to do

Bible study passages
- Matthew 5:3–11
- Matthew 25:31–46
- Luke 10:25–37

Worship
- Psalms: 97; 99; 145
- Hymns: Dear Lord and father of mankind; Seek ye first the kingdom of God.

Activities
- Find ways in which you can put into practice some of the basic principles of the Sermon on the Mount.
- Visit a hospital or care home in your area and see what opportunities there are to connect your experiences with the teaching of Jesus.

Questions for discussion
- What is a parable?
- Where do you see the "kingdom of God" coming today?
- How easy is it to "love your enemies"?

Further reading

Amy-Jill Levine, *Short Stories by Jesus: The Enigmatic Parables of a Controversial Rabbi* (New York: HarperCollins, 2015).

Frank J. Matera, *The Sermon on the Mount: The Perfect Measure of the Christian Life* (Collegeville, MN: Liturgical Press, 2013).

Keith Ward, *Love is His Meaning: Understanding the Teaching of Jesus* (London: SPCK, 2017).

CHAPTER 7

Caesarea Philippi: Decisions,
Decisions . . .

Driving north-east from the Sea of Galilee we soon find ourselves in the Golan Heights, a mountainous area which like the Jordan Valley looks mostly brown and barren. It was taken by the Israelis from Syria in the Six-Day War of June 1967 and is therefore one of Israel's "occupied territories" along with the West Bank. There are very few people living in the Golan Heights, but the area is important for its water. The contemporary political tensions in this area mingle with stunning natural beauty and a rich history.

As we rise in altitude through the Golan Heights, we soon glimpse Mount Hermon with its snow-capped peak. The melting snow from Hermon coupled with several rivers in the region all combine to create the River Jordan further south. Hermon is a landmark mountain rising to over 9,000 feet above sea level. The borders of Syria, Lebanon and Israel all meet at Hermon. There is snow on this mountain all year round, and it attracts tourists from all over the world, who not only ski there but also hike in the nearby Dan Nature Reserve.

After about an hour's drive through the Golan we come to Caesarea Philippi, known today as Banias. It lies on the southern slopes of Hermon in the Israeli occupied area and is familiar from the Gospels. It is the place where Jesus asked his disciples the famous question, "Who do you say that I am?"

Hermon is important in the Bible and is linked with Tabor (Psalm 89:12). Indeed, some of the earliest Christians associated the transfiguration with Hermon because of its closeness to Caesarea Philippi. In the Gospel texts the transfiguration follows the event at Caesarea Philippi. This Caesarea should not be confused with Caesarea Maritima or "Caesarea on the Sea" on the Mediterranean coast. That one had a famous harbour built by Herod the Great. Caesarea Philippi has its own rich and varied history and forms the next Holy Land lens through which we are to look at Lent and our role as disciples of Jesus.

As we enter the site we soon become aware that this is a place of water, greenery and growth. Making our way through the present-day entrance a large body of water reminds us of the history of the place. Imagine we're passing through a gateway of decision. As we ascend steps up to the main area, we find ourselves in an archaeological site with a huge cave at one end. This was the shrine of Pan from which water originally poured out. And along a platform of excavations we can see the remains of further buildings. In the mountain wall numerous niches from ancient buildings are visible, probably originally occupied by statues of gods and goddesses.

Religion and politics

By the time of Jesus in the first century, Caesarea Philippi was already famous for its shrine to the Greek god Pan. There are different stories about Pan, but he was one of many gods and goddesses who developed in Greece and went to the Holy Land with the Greek culture under Alexander the Great in the fourth century BC. Pan was a god of nature associated with the hills, forests and mountains. He was a dancing god evoking sex, fertility and music. He had a tail and horns and was linked with Dionysius, the god of wine. The famous "panpipes" are named after Pan. The name of the place, Banias, comes from the name Pan, and the shrine to him was a water shrine. It must have been based upon a spring in a cave, for it seems that water poured out of a cave area and formed the focus of the shrine. A statue of Pan stood inside the cave, and the shrine was eventually extended outwards. This water shrine to Pan attracted pilgrims from far and wide. It was a cultic centre at which several other gods were probably also invoked.

In the century before Jesus, Herod the Great built a white marble temple in Banias dedicated to the Emperor Augustus. Herod was a master-builder and was responsible for a number of significant constructions around the land, including the temple in Jerusalem and various palaces such as Masada, where he spent time dodging his enemies. Herod was the representative of Rome but is generally reckoned to have been the son of a Jewish father. In any case, he needed to keep the peace with Rome and so built the temple in Banias. It stood alongside the shrine dedicated to Pan so that the power of the Emperor of Rome was now represented alongside the religious shrine. Banias became a centre of both political and religious activity.

In 4 BC Herod the Great died in Jericho and left different parts of the land to his three sons. To Herod Archelaeus he left Judaea, to Herod Antipas he left Galilee, and to Herod Philip he left the area north-east, east and south of the Sea of Galilee including Banias. Herod Philip renamed the area after himself and it became the area belonging to the Caesar Philip, or Caesarea Philippi. Herod Philip turned the place into the capital of the region giving it a further layer of political significance.

During the lifetime of Jesus, then, Caesarea Philippi already had a rich religious and political history. The gods of Greece and Rome were represented by Pan. The Roman Emperor himself was represented by Herod's temple dedicated to him. The natural beauty of the area and, of course, the water made it very desirable. After Herod Philip, the Romans took it over directly. When Jesus got to the region in the 30s of the first century, Caesarea Philippi was alive with religious and political options, challenging everyone who went there. Were they worshippers of Pan or of the Emperor? Were they worshippers of nature and fertility or of the God of Israel? Were they worshippers of worldly power and possession or of some other regime or force?

Caesarea Philippi was a place which provoked response and invited decision, a place that made people think about where their true allegiance lay. No wonder Matthew and Mark among the gospel writers set Jesus' famous question to them here near Caesarea Philippi: "Who do people say that I am?" It was a loaded question which confronted them with major options for their lives. In the Gospels, nothing is said about the significance of the place but an appreciation of its history and significance changes the backdrop to the gospel event and fills out the significance of Jesus' question. In essence, Caesarea Philippi was a place of decision-making, a turning point in faith and allegiance.

Caesarea Philippi in the Gospels

Jesus' question at Caesarea Philippi occurs in all three synoptic Gospels (Matthew 16:13–20; Mark 8:27–33; Luke 9:18–22) though not in John. In Mark's Gospel, the earliest, the event occurs somewhere near the centre of the Gospel. It's usually thought of as a turning point or watershed in the gospel narrative and has the effect of turning the course of events towards Jesus' journey to Jerusalem and all that that will entail. Up to now, the gospel narrative has been predominantly about Jesus preaching the kingdom of God, his teaching in parables and miracles, his healings in Galilee and his ministry around the lake.

Now the story takes us way up north to the "villages of Caesarea Philippi" (Mark 8:27). Matthew says "the district of Caesarea Philippi", and Luke doesn't mention the place at all, possibly indicating that he didn't know of its significance. In Mark and Matthew, it is apparently not actually in Caesarea Philippi but in nearby villages. But in any case, the allusion is there, evoking all the associations mentioned. The leading question is then asked: "Who do people say that I am?" And there are three answers: John the Baptist, Elijah or one of the prophets.

These answers are all significant. John the Baptist (already discussed in Chapter 4) is himself a preacher of repentance and of a specific way of life. He has already played a key role in the beginning of Jesus' ministry and there is already a key association and connection between John and Jesus. Indeed, there has already been another incident which reports that after Herod put John to death some thought that Jesus was John the Baptist come back from the dead (Mark 6:14–29). John, of course, is already associated with the second answer here, Elijah. John is presented somewhat like Elijah in his diet and dress. Elijah was a major prophet who had already himself been involved with a great deal of decision-making as he stood up for Yahweh the God of Israel over against Ba'al. Elijah came out victorious from a confrontation with the prophets of Ba'al on Mount Carmel (1 Kings 18:20–46), fled to Sinai for an encounter with God (19:1–18) and challenged King Ahab and his wife Jezebel in Samaria over a question of injustice (21:1–29).

The third answer is more general: "one of the prophets". The prophets of ancient Israel were people who stood up and spoke out for God usually in the face of social injustice and oppression of the poor. The prophets were God's spokespeople in the community. Elijah and John the Baptist are linked in this respect, and it is not insignificant that people were thinking that Jesus was one of these. And indeed, Jesus is associated with the prophets of Israel and is called a prophet elsewhere in the New Testament (e.g. Matthew 21:11). In Matthew's version of the Caesarea Philippi story he adds Jeremiah to the list of answers about who people think Jesus is. Here, Jeremiah's life of humility and suffering colours the picture. But the point is basically the same: Jesus stands in line with the prophets of ancient Israel.

Next, Jesus asks who the disciples think he is and Peter answers that Jesus is "the Messiah" or "the Christ". This is a powerful word with a long history of meaning and significance in Judaism. The word "messiah" comes from the Hebrew word *mashiach* meaning "anointed one". At its basic level it refers to anyone who is anointed. Being anointed meant having liquid, usually oil, poured over your head with the intention of marking you out for a special role in God's purposes.

In the Old Testament, there are basically three sets of people that get anointed. First, prophets, those who speak the word of God to the people. Elisha, the successor to Elijah, was anointed (1 Kings 19:16). Second, priests such as Aaron were anointed (Exodus 29:7). And finally, the kings of ancient Israel such as Solomon were anointed (1 Kings 1:34). All of these had olive oil, one of the great products of the land from the olive tree, poured over their heads as they were marked out and acknowledged to be special people in God's purposes. In this sense, there were many messiahs. And there were many people who did God's work who were not acknowledged in this way. But there was also expectation of an ideal figure in the future of whom this word might be used. When the Greeks came to translate this word, they used *Christos* or Christ, which is how we get our English word. Of course, this is not Jesus' surname! It is a word used to acknowledge his significance in God's purposes. He is "Jesus, who is the Christ".[29]

Following this "confession" by Peter near Caesarea Philippi, Jesus tells him not to tell anyone. The theme of secrecy runs through Mark's Gospel: on some occasions people know who Jesus is, whilst on others it's kept quiet. It may be that there's a theological reason for this: that the identity of Jesus is something of a mystery. The next section of the text reveals more about Peter and the identity of Jesus. Jesus starts to talk in terms, not of being the Christ, but of being the "Son of Man", another important title in the Old Testament. It could point to Jesus' humanity (as it does when it is used of Ezekiel, e.g. 2:1) or to his status in God's heavenly purposes (as it does in Daniel 7:13). But in any case, it is Jesus' preferred title and carries with it an element of suffering. It is certainly not the worldly, political figure that Peter probably means when he calls Jesus the Messiah.

By the end of this incident near Caesarea Philippi, Peter is being rejected for misunderstanding the meaning of the words he has used. Peter rebukes Jesus for talking about suffering, but Jesus says, "Get behind me, Satan! For you are setting your mind not on divine things but on human things" (Mark 8:33). There is more to Jesus' mission than Peter can even imagine.

Living the decisions

The question now arises: "what meaning does Caesarea Philippi have for Christians today?" In one sense, of course, this text is one of the easiest in the Gospels: a straightforward request for a decision. It certainly boils down to whether we will be followers of Jesus or not. However, the question that Jesus asks his disciples, "Who do you say that I am?", is often taken by modern Christians as if it's a matter of intellectual assent to a particular view. That is, it could mean, "Do you think Jesus is the Messiah or the Christ?" The question is often put to mean, "Do you think Jesus is the Son of God?" or "Do you think Jesus was really human and divine?" It might mean, "Is Jesus your saviour?" or, "Do you think Jesus was God incarnate as opposed to just a good man?" There are many options like these that are often bandied about to test people's belief.

And all of these are very important questions for Christians today but I don't think this is what Jesus was asking in the gospel story near Caesarea Philippi. Too often today, we think that questions of belief are the real heart of faith: accepting that something is the case about Jesus. But at Caesarea Philippi, whatever else Jesus is asking, he is inviting his disciples to follow his lifestyle, his way of living. Indeed Peter, who seems to get the answer correct (Jesus is the "Christ"), has little idea what the words actually mean. He has some idea of what being with Jesus involves but hasn't yet got the message about the life he is being invited into and the difference it should make. He hasn't yet seen the connection with Jesus' journey to the cross and to death.

In 1943 the German pastor and theologian Dietrich Bonhoeffer was arrested and imprisoned for his anti-Nazi activities. In 1945 he was executed by hanging in Flossenbürg concentration camp. During his time in a cell at Tegel military prison Bonhoeffer wrote what later became his *Letters and Papers from Prison* in which he asked his famous question, "What is bothering me incessantly is the question what Christianity really is, or indeed who Christ really is, for us today".[30] Bonhoeffer's question is essentially the question Jesus put to his disciples at Caesarea Philippi. But Bonhoeffer would never have been thinking merely of a view of Christ's identity or what words were most appropriate. His understanding of the meaning of Christ was a matter of life and death. Too often, especially in the western world, Christians see following Jesus in terms of belief rather than of life style.

But Caesarea Philippi the place helps focus the question in the story. It is the location, as we have seen, that makes Jesus' question more poignant. The place was a place of natural beauty, of political tension, of the power of other gods and of worldly gods, of idols and all manner of options vying for allegiance. The setting still has its impact today as the question comes to us. Do we say that Jesus is Lord among the many options in our own day? It is always possible that the temptations of the modern age will become our personal gods: money, material possessions, sex, nature, professional power, influence or success. The Caesarea Philippi question focuses the mind and the heart on what we are most concerned about and what matters to us ultimately. It is at this level that both the place and the text of the Caesarea Philippi event ask us where our true allegiance lies today. Are we true followers of Jesus? Are we really his disciples? Or not?

Two other thoughts. First, the answer to this question of allegiance is often unknown even to ourselves. Our own deepest motives can be a mystery to us. This is why discernment of our inner motives is crucial to our faith. We need to examine and reflect upon what drives us and motivates us. The second thing is that we're deceived if we think that doing religious things always amounts to following Jesus. Some of the worst inversions of faith can be found in religion. Typically, we can think that attending church or doing things for the church amounts to being a disciple of Jesus. Sometimes people who do the most for the church are still a long way off from real discipleship. And this is not to judge them, but just to say that if we think we are "saving ourselves" by more and more religiosity, we are probably wrong. We go to church more, read the Bible more, go on retreats and read more religious books. But this isn't what Jesus had in mind near Caesarea Philippi. It's more a question of "are we following the lifestyle of Jesus, living a life of caring for others, a life of compassion, humility and healing?"

Conclusion

Caesarea Philippi is a turning point, a watershed, a place of decision and response to Jesus and ultimately to God. We have encountered this pattern of presence and response throughout this study. Reflecting on particular moments such as Jesus' baptism and our own baptisms brought us to the doorway of decision in Advent. Now in Lent, Caesarea Philippi brings us to a particular moment of commitment. We have discerned God's presence in Jesus. It is now time to ask ourselves who we say he is, not just what we make of him or what title or word might most appropriately sum him up.

It's now time to ask ourselves whether Jesus is more important than all the other contenders on the smorgasbord of modern life. It's time to ask whether he is our priority concern. Is he the one who focuses everything else we do? Is he the one we follow ultimately and what does that mean? Caesarea Philippi and Lent are about Christian discipleship and what sort of disciples we will be. And it may be that the question about who Jesus is for us should be asked not just once but daily.[31]

Things to do

Bible study passages
- 1 Kings 18:20–46
- 1 Kings 21:1–29
- Matthew 16:13–20; Mark 8:27–33; Luke 9:18–22

Worship
- Psalms: 8; 119:97–112; 146
- Hymns: Just as I am without one plea; I, the Lord of sea and sky.

Activities
- What decisions have you made recently, major and minor? What are your decision-making processes? Make a note of these.
- Talk to others about their decision-making processes.

Questions for discussion
- What has changed in your understanding of Jesus' question at Caesarea Philippi?
- What does "following Jesus" mean today?
- What is the difference between a "belief" and a "life style"?

Further reading
Alister McGrath, *Mere Discipleship: On Growing in Wisdom and Hope* (London: SPCK, 2018).

John Pritchard, *Living Faithfully: Following Christ in Everyday Life* (London: SPCK, 2013).

Samuel Wells, *How Then Shall We Live? Christian Engagement with Contemporary Issues* (Norwich: Canterbury Press, 2016).

CHAPTER 8

Mount Tabor: Transfiguration

Mount Tabor is the mountain of Jesus' transfiguration in Galilee. It rises 1,600 feet above the Jezreel Valley and 1,900 feet above sea level. It is unique for several reasons, one of which is its seemingly perfect, rounded shape visible for miles around. From every angle, from every road and from every altitude it is somehow easily identifiable once you know it. It looks perfectly cropped and separate with a character all its own. The mountain has always had an engaging mystique. It's always been a holy mountain. Until recently the way up the hairpin road felt quite perilous. Now, walls and better road surfaces make the journey somewhat smoother than it once was. Christian pilgrims travel up by taxi or hike. And modern Israelis paraglide from the top.

Let's go on a journey to the summit of this unusual mountain. As we ascend and the altitude changes, we're literally aware of a modification in consciousness. Imagine you're walking up with Jesus and he's telling you of his message and ministry. You're doubtful and sceptical, wondering what he's really talking about. As you rise you become apprehensive and frightened. You feel like going back down but you're with him and want to remain committed. The "point of no return" hits you with a deepening sense of wanting to see things through to the end but you still don't understand. You're determined to stay the course, but you have your doubts. Then you start to see things differently. From the top the views of the surrounding area are stunning, but you're exhausted.

Visible from just about everywhere on the mountain today is the huge Basilica of the Transfiguration designed by the famous Holy Land architect Antonio Barluzzi in 1924. It's a massive barn of a place built in light brown stone and capturing superbly a sense of holiness and transfiguration. Entering, you settle down in a seat at the back. It's a simple austere building, not overly decorated, with the high altar set down lower than the rest of the church. A mosaic of the transfiguration shines out from the apse and there are stained-glass windows depicting scenes from the Book of Revelation. At the back of the church there are two chapels, one dedicated to Moses and one to Elijah. This church somehow breathes the story as well as the experience of transfiguration.

The sense at the top of the mountain is one of presence and mystery. Things look different from here. It's another turning point. There's no doubt about it: Tabor has a profound and moving effect, triggering a different awareness and mood. It provides our next Holy Land lens for Lent.

Tabor and Megiddo

The views from the top of Mount Tabor are breathtaking, especially on a clear day. Sometimes Mount Hermon can be seen in the distance with its glistening white snow peaks. There's also sometimes an amazing view of the Rift Valley and across to Jordan. The surrounding Valley of Jezreel or Plain of Esdraelon is also visible for miles around. And not far away Mount Megiddo can sometimes be seen. This is one of the most important mountains in the area and a place where hundreds of battles have taken place. So much is Megiddo associated with warfare that it has become symbolic of all battles and the place in the Book of Revelation where the final battle will take place (16:16). From the Hebrew *Har Megiddo* or Mount Megiddo, we get "Armageddon". Megiddo stands in stark contrast to Tabor: warfare versus transfiguration.

It is probable that Tabor was always important with its sense of mystery and its views of the surrounding area. It seems always to have had religious and political significance and, like a number of mountains in Galilee, was a strategic location for seeing oncoming enemies. This mountain was already important in the Old Testament when, in the days of the Judges, Deborah and Barak (leader of her army in Judges 4) rally their men at this mountain and go into battle with Jabin, King of Hazor, and Sisera (leader of his army). Sisera's army is defeated and Sisera flees alone. As he comes to the tent of Heber the Kenite, who has broken his allegiance to the King of Hazor, he is invited in by Heber's wife Jael, who drives a tent peg through his temple, killing him while he is asleep. She then hands him over to Deborah and Barak. Nestling at the bottom of the mountain today is a village called Daboriya after Deborah the Judge. This famous Old Testament story tells of war and death. But it is goodness and God's transforming power that came to be Tabor's key associations.

We know of the transfiguration of Jesus from the Gospels of Matthew, Mark and Luke. Jesus takes his inner group of disciples, Peter, James and John, up the mountain, and there he is transfigured before them. His face and garments shine brightly and the disciples' sense of him changes. From here on, they begin to see something different about his purposes. As we have seen, in the early days of Christianity, the transfiguration was remembered as having taken place at Mount Hermon in the same location as Caesarea Philippi. As the transfiguration follows Caesarea Philippi in the synoptic Gospels, it seemed likely that Hermon was the mountain of transfiguration. The Old Testament had already linked Hermon and Tabor (Psalm 89:12) and both were acknowledged as important symbolic mountains. But it was not long before the transfiguration was also remembered in Jerusalem at the Mount of Olives, a place particularly associated with the coming of God and his messiah. By the fourth century the transfiguration was also associated with Tabor.

We don't know exactly how soon there was a church building at Tabor, but pilgrims from the early Byzantine period bear witness to churches there by the sixth century. They were probably destroyed in the early Muslim period in the seventh century. When the Crusader kingdom was established in the Holy Land in the late eleventh century, they built a Benedictine monastery on the mountain and a defensive wall around the top. For centuries, different regimes have held power at Tabor, both Christian and Muslim. But from the fourth century onwards, Tabor was established as the place of Jesus' transfiguration. And from that time, Christian pilgrims have made their way there to reflect upon the meaning of this extraordinary event.

As we enter the site at the top of the mountain and make our way towards the basilica, we pass through some of the remains of the Crusader monastery which are still visible. There is a powerful sense of history and religious awe on this mountain, a sense of the numinous. Today,

Tabor is looked after by the Franciscan community, and it is possible
with appropriate arrangements to make a retreat there. The mountain is
visited by thousands of pilgrims every year.

The transfiguration in the Gospels

The story of Jesus' transfiguration in the Gospels is perhaps one of the
most difficult to understand. It occurs in all three synoptics (Matthew
17:1–8; Mark 9:2–8; Luke 9:28–36) though not in John. This is interesting
in itself, but it is often pointed out that the whole of John's Gospel is about
transfiguration. Even so, the story occurs only in the three Gospels, and
like Caesarea Philippi is another important turning point in them all.
In the eastern churches the transfiguration of Jesus is one of the main
subjects of the icons, and the theme is central to Orthodox theology,
spirituality and worship.

The symbolism of Moses and Elijah in this story connects it with
Sinai and the events of the Exodus (Exodus 24 and 33–34). These
consist of powerful theophanies or appearances of God to Moses. There
Moses goes to the mountain with three companions and God appears
in a cloud. Many of the themes in Exodus appear in the transfiguration
story and the gospel writers have clearly based their accounts of the
Transfiguration on the accounts of God's appearances to Moses. The
theology of the Covenant at Mount Sinai, the giving of the Law and
the Ten Commandments and the formation of the people of Israel is
also carried over into the transfiguration accounts. 1 Kings 19 tells of
the appearance of God to Elijah at Horeb or Sinai, and this also forms
part of the background. At the Monastery of St Catherine at the foot of
Mount Sinai in Egypt, the church is dedicated to the transfiguration, and
a sixth-century mosaic of the event fills the apse.

The transfiguration story has sometimes been thought of as a
resurrection appearance story projected back into the narrative of the
Gospels. It is perhaps better seen as a foretaste or glimpse of what is
to come, providing a shaft of insight pointing forward to the cross and
resurrection. Following the events at Caesarea Philippi when the disciples
have been faced with the major question about who Jesus is, they are

taken to the top of a mountain. In fact, it's only the inner group of Peter, James and John. On the mountain, they see Jesus transfigured. The word is *metamorphosis*, a change of form. Jesus' garments shine brightly, reminding us of Moses' face shining in the Exodus account. The cloud and the voice are also reminiscent of Moses' encounter. Elijah and Moses appear and are in conversation with Jesus, perhaps suggesting dialogue between the Jewish past and the emerging new regime of Jesus. Peter wants to make three booths for them and doesn't understand what is going on.

Then the cloud, and the voice announces that God is appointing Jesus to a key role in his purposes. The voice says, "This is my Son, the Beloved; listen to him!" (Mark 9:7), connecting the event with Jesus' baptism, where he has been announced as God's son at the beginning of his ministry. Now it is announced to all present as his ministry deepens. At the end of Mark's account, there is only Jesus left. He has fulfilled everything associated with Moses and Elijah, establishing a new covenant, a new law and a new people. The disciples have seen something new about Jesus that they hadn't seen before. And he has entered a new phase in his journey to Jerusalem.

Both Matthew and Luke take up Mark's transfiguration story and there are some interesting variations bringing out some different emphases in what is basically the same event. Matthew's account is close to Mark's, but he adds that Jesus' face really did shine like the sun, and his garments were white as light. The cloud also shines. There is more shining in this account, and the connection with Moses is even stronger. Peter addresses Jesus as Lord, and the disciples fall on their faces. Jesus invites them to get up and not to be afraid. Again, the event is attached to the baptism of Jesus by the voice, and to the resurrection where the guards fall down as if dead (Matthew 28:1–10).

In Luke there are other emphases. Here, Jesus goes up the mountain to pray. His face is changed rather than shining but his clothes are dazzling white. Moses and Elijah are now "in glory" (Luke 9:31), recalling the glory of Exodus 33. It looks as though they are not so much superseded as established firmly as the basis of the experience that Jesus now takes further. A conversation between them all now tells of Jesus' own "exodus", connecting the transfiguration again with the events of the Exodus. Jesus' own journey to the cross is now effectively a "new exodus". Luke also mentions Jerusalem as Jesus' destination: it is the continuing location of God's activity in history. Moses and Elijah then depart and even though they have been glorified by Jesus, he overtakes them.

Clearly something very significant has happened on the Mountain of Transfiguration. Jesus himself has changed as his own deepening awareness of his place in God's purposes has dawned upon him. But the disciples' perception of Jesus has also moved. They have seen something different about his identity and purpose. And the context must be noted again: the transfiguration story follows the Caesarea Philippi question, and it is as though this experience on the mountain is Jesus' own answer to the question about who he is. The experience on the mountain is followed in each Gospel by the account of the healing of the epileptic boy, which suggests further that the effects of the transfiguration include healing (e.g. Mark 9:14–29).

And this points to the wider context and emphasis of this strange and mysterious event. Wrapped up in references to Jesus' suffering as the "Son of Man", it tells of the transfiguration of suffering and the healing of sickness. This message fans out across the Gospels with powerful associations and consequences pointing forward to the cross and resurrection. No wonder the transfiguration has been so fundamental to Christian theology, worship and spirituality down the centuries and remains so today.

Transfiguring life

In view of the importance of the transfiguration of Jesus in the Gospels and in the Christian tradition, what can be said about its continuing meaning for Christians today? What difference does the transfiguration make to Christian faith? First of all, we must not think of the events of the Gospels as being simply "about Jesus". We must think of them as relating to the whole of life and indeed of creation. The technical way of putting this is that Christology is fundamentally connected to creation and is on a continuum with it. Things pertaining to Christology or to Jesus affect our thinking about the rest of God's dealing with the world and human life. Transfiguration, then, is linked up with the possibilities for creation and human life. This is why this event in the Gospels has been considered to be so precious, especially in the Christian East. It's about the way God deals with the world as seen through Jesus.

In this section, therefore, we will be thinking about the way the transfiguration can be thought of as a paradigm for transfiguring the world. At the practical level the question is simply this: how can we transfigure or play a part in transfiguring the world, our countries, societies, communities and families? The question is practical and political. Answers might range from our personal treatment of other people to playing a part in local or national politics. There are many organizations that might sum up quickly the type of work in mind here: Oxfam, the Children's Society, Christian Aid or your local hospice. The work of hospitals, care homes, educational institutions and churches would also feature. Through them people's lives are improved, developed and transformed. This is work for the kingdom of God, transfiguring the world and the people in it. Our work in these places joins in with God's own work and purposes.

Two powerful examples of transfiguration come from the Holy Land today. The first is two of the many peace projects that operate within the Holy Land. Transfiguring life in the Holy Land requires an understanding of the problem and involves addressing pain and suffering. The current conflict in the Holy Land is quite recent. People often think it goes back centuries, but it can really only be traced back to the nineteenth century, the establishment of the State of Israel in 1948 and the occupation of East Jerusalem and the West Bank in the Six-Day War of 1967.[32]

Through all these waves of change Jews and Palestinians have come into conflict with each other through the emergence of different stories or narratives about their identities. In a situation often likened to South Africa and Northern Ireland, Israel–Palestine has been the scene of tragic and horrific violence and misunderstanding of who the two sides living in the same country actually are. Although the conflict is not strictly between Israelis and Palestinians (there are a million Palestinians in Israel who are Israelis themselves), but rather between Israelis and West Bankers, there are layers of misunderstanding and prejudice leading to repeated cases of violence and attack on each other.

My first example of transfiguring life, then, comes from two organizations which work for peace in a number of locations. The first is Seeds of Peace which was founded in 1993 and organizes summer camps for teenagers in Maine in the USA. It operates in a number of conflict zones throughout the world, not just in Israel–Palestine. The second is an organization called Kids4Peace founded in the Anglican Diocese of Jerusalem in the mid-1990s. This has developed into running summer camps for children in Europe, Canada and elsewhere as well as in the USA. Both these organizations have brought together children from both sides of the conflict in the Holy Land to enable them to experience their so-called "enemies" on neutral ground. There are staggering stories of mutual understanding and reconciliation, indeed life-long friendship, emerging. It's as if the lens of violence and revenge has been taken away and "the other" has been seen in a new light. Lives have been changed and transfigured.

My second example is the orchestra founded by the Israeli Jewish conductor and pianist Daniel Barenboim. Barenboim is an Argentinian Jewish musician with Israeli citizenship. He joined with his long-time friend, the Palestinian literary critic and author Edward Said, to form the West-Eastern Divan Orchestra This project is an orchestra that welcomes both Israelis and Palestinians into its ranks as a way of enabling both sides of the conflict to encounter and listen to each other. Barenboim insists that he is no politician, but that music can change the way we see the world and that his orchestra can change the way the musicians see each other. As in the previous example there are stories of new friendships, of new understanding, and of the elimination of mistrust and fear. Primarily through learning to listen to each other, which all musicians must do, Barenboim believes music can change the world. Indeed, through a powerful instrument like this orchestra, the world might even be transfigured. The Barenboim-Said Akademie has recently been set up in Berlin and has the same agenda. In all of this, we see something of God's transfiguring action in the world through the work of human beings.

Conclusion

Mount Tabor in Galilee is the mountain of Jesus' transfiguration. We have been to the top and seen something new. Perceptions have changed and insights have dawned. Things don't look the same from here as they once did. In this chapter Tabor has been the Lenten lens through which we have looked at the transfiguration in the Gospels and at its implications for the task of transfiguring the world in which we live today. For disciples who have seen this shimmering vision of God's presence in Jesus, the challenge is to bring about such changes in the world that families, communities and societies are re-channelled towards health, harmony and peace. We have seen various examples and possibilities of this. It's up to us now to identify and contribute to this process wherever and whenever we can.

Transfiguring life is the business of Christian discipleship once you have seen God in Jesus and decided to follow him. This is the dawning of the kingdom, pointing forward to new creation and resurrection. It's a natural progression from Caesarea Philippi to Mount Tabor, avoiding and eliminating the horrors of Megiddo and everything associated with it.[33] Having glimpsed this transfiguring element of Jesus' life and message at Tabor, we turn now to the final sections of our journey: the Last Supper, and Jesus' death and resurrection in Jerusalem.

Things to do

Bible study passages
- Exodus 24:15–18
- Exodus 33:17–23
- Matthew 17:1–8; Mark 9:2–8; Luke 9:28–36

Worship
- Psalms: 27; 72; 150
- Hymns: 'Tis good, Lord, to be here; Lord, the light of your love is shining.

Activities
- Try doing a walk or a hike somewhere. How does your sense of things change?
- Find a way in which you can contribute to "transfiguring" the world through helping an individual or volunteering in an institution.

Questions for discussion
- What parallels are there between the stories about Moses and the transfiguration of Jesus?
- What do you understand by "transfiguration"?
- What sense does it make to talk about "transfiguring the world"?

Further reading

Daniel Barenboim, *Everything is Connected: The Power of Music* (London: Phoenix, 2009).

Dorothy Lee, *Transfiguration* (London: Continuum, 2004).

Kenneth Stevenson, *Rooted in Detachment: Living the Transfiguration* (London: DLT, 2007).

CHAPTER 9

Jerusalem: The Last Supper

We began our journey at the beginning of Advent in Jerusalem at the Temple Mount where Jesus spoke of his body as the real temple. Now, as we approach Easter, we return to Jerusalem for the final two weeks, focusing on the Last Supper and the death and resurrection of Jesus.

Our penultimate Lenten lens from the Holy Land is the so-called Cenacle on Mount Zion. Known to pilgrims as the room of the Last Supper, the name comes from the Italian word *cenaculum* meaning "dining room". Come with me in your imagination on a winding walk through the narrow streets of the Old City of Jerusalem, through markets and shops and round about towards the Zion Gate. The Cenacle is located on Mount Zion in the area of David's Tomb and the Benedictine Dormition Abbey just outside today's Old City walls. Following the road around to the Cenacle, you begin to think of what the Last Supper might really have been like.

Mount Zion and the Cenacle are on the south-western side of Jerusalem. The name Zion has been used over the centuries to refer to different parts of the city as well as to the whole. In Hebrew, it means "dry" or "thirsty". Today, Mount Zion is a somewhat indeterminate area stretching inside and outside the Old City walls. With a variety of buildings both ancient and modern, the area is busy with traffic. Pilgrims and tourists rush around to see the sights. Zion was inside the walls of Jesus' day. But, in any case, this general area is probably where he ate the meal with his disciples the night before he died.

When we arrive at the Cenacle, we ascend some stone steps and enter the room. It's quite large with a high ceiling. In the sixteenth century it was turned into a mosque, and the niche in the wall pointing in the direction of Mecca is still clearly visible. The stonework is a light brown colour. Suddenly you notice the typical Crusader arches supporting the ceiling up above. These are from the twelfth century, and so this cannot literally be the room of the Last Supper. It's not old enough! The history of the building is complex and stretches back centuries, but the room itself can only be said to be where the meal that Jesus ate with his disciples has been remembered over the last thousand years or so. It is, of course, possible that the meal itself took place in a room in this vicinity, but that's about as close as we can get. The Gospels tell us nothing about the location of the meal. Mount Zion itself, and indeed the area of the Last Supper room, has also been associated with the coming of the Holy Spirit at Pentecost, and so you come to appreciate another major connection as well.

As we focus on the Last Supper in this chapter, imagine yourself in the busy part of an eastern city where a meal is being prepared at the time of the Passover festival of the Jews. What sort of a meal was it? Unlike the well-known painting of the event by Leonardo Da Vinci with Jesus and the disciples sitting along one side of a long table, it's more likely that they reclined on the floor around three sides of a dining area. This was the style of eating during the Roman period. Imagine yourself at such a meal with waiters bringing in food and drink on the fourth side and guests passing it around.

The Passover meal

There may be something of a mystery about the exact location of the Last Supper, but we know much more about the meal itself. The Passover meal in Judaism goes back to the earliest times and lies at the heart of the Jewish faith even today. The celebration looks backwards as well as forwards, capturing Jewish identity as it has been in the past and will continue to be in the future. We learn about the Passover meal in Exodus 12–13. The history of the traditions is rich and varied, but as far as the text is concerned we know that during ancient Israel's period of slavery in Egypt and at the time of their leaving Egypt, God established a sacrifice and a meal. An unblemished lamb was to be sacrificed and the blood would be put on the doorposts of the Israelites so that God would "pass over" those houses and not destroy the Israelites when he destroyed the Egyptians in their houses.

The meal itself would be of unleavened bread because the people would be in a hurry to leave Egypt and would have no time to leaven their bread. It became known as the "bread of haste". There would also be wine, bitter herbs and other elements. As the tradition developed, a set procedure emerged with the lighting of candles, eating of bread and cups of wine. The meal as outlined in Exodus was commanded by God to be an annual event celebrated for ever in commemoration of what he had done for them in bringing them out of slavery. It was a meal celebrating the end of oppression and the beginning of freedom and liberation through the events of the Exodus. It was a meal that for centuries to come would bring to mind the Jews' identity as the liberated people of God.

The Passover meal was not strictly speaking an atonement meal, because God was not passing over the Israelites' sin but passing over their houses in order to save them from physical destruction. Nevertheless, it was a foundational meal which gave them their specific identity. The well-known question of the youngest son of the family, "why is this night different from all other nights?" has its roots in Exodus (12:26–27) and is still asked at the meal today. It is the cue for the father of the family to tell his children the story of the Jewish people and their liberation.

Passover was celebrated every year in Jerusalem, and we know from the Gospels that Jesus chose to go to Jerusalem at the time of the festival. The meal he ate with his disciples the night before he died was most likely a Passover meal reinterpreted in terms of his own life and death. For Christians, therefore, Exodus, Passover and the Last Supper are all closely bound up together.

The Last Supper in the Gospels and Paul

The Last Supper, as it is now known, occurs in all four Gospels, although it is somewhat different in John (Matthew 26:17–30; Mark 14:12–26; Luke 22:7–39; John 13:1–38). It also occurs in Paul's first letter to the Corinthians, Chapter 11. However, there are different details and emphases among these accounts.

The Gospels

In the synoptic Gospels, there is little doubt that the Last Supper is a Passover meal. There has been a great deal of scholarly work on this in the last century, and it is mostly agreed that Jesus ate a Passover meal with his disciples before going out and being arrested and then crucified the next day. There were certainly several different types of meal in Judaism at the time, and there could have been other meals during Passover, so we must be clear what we mean.

The first three Gospels indicate that the meal was a Passover meal. Mark says that it was, "On the first day of Unleavened Bread, when the Passover lamb is sacrificed" (14:12) that Jesus sent two disciples into the city to prepare a place for him to eat the meal. This day was the day when people got their lamb sacrificed for the meal that evening. In the synoptics, therefore, it looks as though the lambs are sacrificed, then the meal takes place and then Jesus is crucified the following day. The Passover festival would have taken place in the month equivalent to our April / May. It was a month called Nisan, and the day itself was the fourteenth of the month.

In John's Gospel, however, things are somewhat different, and it is clear that the meal eaten by Jesus with his disciples takes place a day earlier. We are told that it was "before the festival of the Passover" (13:1). It looks as though the author of the Fourth Gospel has changed the chronology of the last days of Jesus' life in order to have him die at the time the Passover lambs were dying, that is on the afternoon before (not after, as in the synoptics) the meal was eaten. This shift in the order of events is usually reckoned to have a theological motive: the theology of Jesus the Lamb of God. It is at the beginning of this Gospel that Jesus is called "the Lamb of God" (1:29, 36).

This then means that John's Last Supper meal is not strictly speaking a Passover meal but a meal at the time of Passover. The question is made more fascinating by the fact that in John's narrative, although a meal is referred to, there is no bread and wine mentioned, and the focus of the whole event is on Jesus washing his disciples' feet. Here the message is primarily about humility and service, a theme John has in common with Luke.

The probable theological motive in John's chronology makes it look as though the synoptics are historically more reliable: the Last Supper was indeed a Passover meal with all the associations already mentioned. It was a meal about freedom and liberation from slavery in Egypt. It was a meal that continued to remember and to relive on an annual basis the identity of the Jewish people. By going to Jerusalem at Passover time and eating the meal with his disciples Jesus was very clearly associating himself and his coming death with the traditions and meanings of Passover. This becomes clear in the "words of institution", as they are often called: "this is my body", "this is my blood".

Paul

The earliest account of the Last Supper in the New Testament comes to us in Paul's first letter to the Corinthians (11:23–34). This is a lively and fast-moving pastoral letter from Paul to the Christians in Corinth written in the middle of the first century, before the Gospels. In the early part of the letter, Paul is clear about the importance of Christ's crucifixion and resurrection but also uses the imagery of the Passover for Jesus. In 5:7–8 he writes, "For our paschal lamb, Christ, has been sacrificed. Therefore, let us celebrate the festival, not with the old yeast, the yeast of malice and evil, but with the unleavened bread of sincerity and truth." Here, Paul interprets Christ through the metaphor of the Passover with its unleavened bread. Christ is now the Passover (paschal) lamb who is put to death. Effectively, Paul sees Jesus as the new Passover, and although he does not mention it again, his view is clear: Jesus himself took the Passover meal and reinterpreted it in terms of his own death.

A number of things emerge from 1 Corinthians 11:23–34. First, Paul is delivering to the Corinthians what he has already received. This is usually taken to mean that his narrative of the Last Supper probably goes back to the Jerusalem Church. He also says that the Corinthians are eating and drinking the bread and wine in a disorderly way and therefore bringing judgement upon themselves and "profaning the body and blood of the Lord" (v. 27 Revised Standard Version). A number of different meal types may have influenced the celebration in Corinth, and the Christian meal may have been celebrated within the context of

an ordinary meal. Paul writes to advise the Corinthians to be orderly
in their celebration, reminding them that they are celebrating a meal
with deeply serious spiritual significance. Paul might give us the oldest
narrative of the Last Supper (including, "This is my body that is for you.
Do this in remembrance of me" and "This cup is the new covenant in
my blood. Do this, as often as you drink it, in remembrance of me")
but we do not yet have the later developed notions of real presence or
transubstantiation here.

It looks near certain that Jesus celebrated the Passover meal with
his disciples the night before he died. The Gospels have different
interpretations, but the connection is clear: at the Last Supper Jesus took
the Jewish Passover meal and reinterpreted it in terms of himself. Earlier
on, Paul had already used the idea of the Passover lamb to interpret the
significance of Jesus. In view of all this, then, how are we to understand
the meal that lies at the heart of a great deal of Christian worship today?

The Eucharist today

During Lent and especially Holy Week, it is appropriate to ask ourselves
how we think of the Eucharist today. One important thing about it, which
even many Christians miss, is that it is basically a meal. Wrapped up as it
is in the Jewish traditions of Exodus and Passover, it is best understood
primarily as a meal.

Among the many churches, the service based on the meal has different
names, such as Holy Communion, the Lord's Supper, the Breaking of
Bread, the Mass, the Liturgy of the Sacrament or the Eucharist. It can
also look and be very different on different occasions and in different
traditions. At the Orthodox and Roman Catholic end of the spectrum the
service is usually very ornate visibly, with music, vestments, candles and
incense. At the other end of the spectrum in the Methodist and Baptist
churches, for example, there will be little if any such aesthetic decoration.
The theology, spirituality and understanding of the Eucharist also vary
across the different churches.

In many cases, interpretations of the Eucharist have developed in
opposition to other interpretations, such as the views that emerged during

the Reformation in the sixteenth century. In this section, we shall briefly consider some of the possible understandings of the service, emphasizing its fundamental significance as a meal.

The main interpretations might be summed up using the following words: real presence, transubstantiation, consubstantiation and sacrament. It is clear that there isn't a single view of the Last Supper in the New Testament or in the Christian tradition. In the New Testament there is no detailed explanation of what the meal means. And it is clear from 1 Corinthians that the Christian celebration took place in the context of an ordinary meal. Scholars have recently noted that other meals in the Graeco-Roman world also influenced the Christian celebration. In the early centuries there was a gradual development of the idea that the Eucharist was attached to the incarnation and that Jesus was really present in the meal. In due course, his real presence became associated specifically with the bread and wine.

But it was not until the ninth century that the details about this became specific. A controversy between two Benedictine monks at the monastery of Corbie in Northern France focused the issues. Radbertus wrote a treatise on the Lord's Supper saying that the elements of bread and wine could be identified with Jesus' body and blood. His opponent in the same monastery, Ratramnus, disagreed, claiming that there was a difference between the elements and the body and blood of Christ. From this controversy emerged the view stated at the Fourth Lateran Council (1215) to the effect that Jesus is truly present in the elements at the Mass.

The wider medieval debate came to a head in the theology of Thomas Aquinas (1225–1274). He used the philosophy of Aristotle (384–322 BC) to form his view of "transubstantiation". Aquinas claimed that there are two elements in everything that exists: the inner "substance" and the outer "accidents" or things accidental to them. A chair, for example, has its inner substance which makes it a chair, and also its accidental elements such as blue or brown, hard or soft. In bread, therefore, there is the inner substance which makes it bread and its outer accidental elements such as brown or white, hard or soft.

Aquinas' claim is that at the words of consecration in the Mass the inner substances of the bread and wine change into the body and blood of Christ, while the outer accidental aspects, the appearances, remain unchanged. This is a transference or "carrying across" (*trans*) of substance. The doctrine of transubstantiation remains the official teaching about the Mass in the Roman Catholic Church, but it was one of the key controversial features in the period of the Reformation.

The leaders of the Reformation had their own views. One of the main ones came from Huldrich Zwingli (1484–1531) in Zurich. He claimed that the elements at the Eucharist should be taken symbolically rather than literally and that the bread and wine were symbols like a wedding ring: they carry the meaning but are not themselves the thing signified. In the same period, Martin Luther (1483 -1546) put forward a view known as "consubstantiation", that is that there are two substances present together in the elements, one substance "with" (*con*) the other. In this view both the substance of the bread and wine and the substance of Christ's body and blood are present together in the bread and wine.

The final word, sacrament, is used widely with different emphases. In general, a sacrament is a specific place where God is revealed. The word is used by Christians both of the Eucharist in general and of the bread and wine in particular. The word emphasizes that this meal is a particular place where God is made known and where Jesus is present. The notion of the Eucharist as a sacrament can be found in the Orthodox Churches and also in the Anglican Church, which speaks of a sacrament as "an outward and visible sign of an inward and spiritual grace".[34] Sacrament is a powerful but perhaps less specific word than the others.

All these interpretations of the Eucharist have their basis in understanding it as a meal and indeed without this fundamental concept none of the other interpretations make complete sense. An ordinary meal is a place of sharing, encounter and communion, a place where we communicate with each other and with God. The Eucharist is an extraordinary, sacramental meal with all the traditions of Exodus, Passover and the Last Supper bound into it. It is the Christian meal of liberation.

Conclusion

The room of the Last Supper in Jerusalem, the Cenacle, has turned our minds to associated texts in the Gospels and in the writings of the apostle Paul. Once again, we have glimpsed the presence of God in a particular moment in Jesus' life. His last meal with his disciples was probably a Passover meal, which he reinterpreted in terms of his own life and death. Soon the event was celebrated as the central Christian service. Jesus himself was thought of as being present generally in the meal and subsequently in the bread and wine themselves.

Different interpretations of this celebration developed and have sadly divided Christians from each other. But the key thing to grasp is the nature of the celebration as a family meal in which Christians come together and participate in the presence of God and of Jesus in a special way. Having experienced and celebrated the presence, we then go out to live a life of discipleship and love.[35]

Things to do

Bible study passages
- Exodus 12:1–42
- Matthew 26:17–30; Mark 14:12–26; Luke 22:7–39; John 13:1–38
- 1 Corinthians 11:23–34

Worship
- Psalms: 113; 114; 115
- Hymns: O thou, who at thy Eucharist didst pray; Give thanks with a grateful heart.

Activities
- Attend a Eucharist in two or three different churches to experience the similarities and differences.
- Get your minister or priest to celebrate an informal Eucharist with participants reclining around a low table.

Questions for discussion

- What is the Passover background to the Eucharist?
- Was the Last Supper a Passover meal or not?
- What does the Eucharist mean in your church?

Further reading

Andrew Davison, *Why Sacraments?* (London: SPCK, 2013).

Brant Pitre and Scott Hahn, *Jesus and the Jewish Roots of the Eucharist: Unlocking the Secrets of the Last Supper* (New York: Image, 2016).

Ben Witherington III, *Making a Meal of It: Rethinking the Theology of the Lord's Supper* (Waco, TX: Baylor University Press, 2007).

Jerusalem: Death and Resurrection

The nine previous chapters of this book have taken us to some key places in the Holy Land, enabled a closer look at some well-known gospel texts, and led us through some major stages of Christian faith and life. Now, in this final chapter, we are in Jerusalem again and our Holy Land lens is the Church of the Holy Sepulchre where we consider Good Friday and Easter.

Come with me once more through one of the main gates of the Old City to find this church deep inside the Christian Quarter. As before, we walk through winding streets and alleyways, vibrant market stalls, coffee shops and crowds of people. It's a maze of dizzying sensory experiences of all kinds. Eventually, we pass through an archway marked "Holy Sepulchre" and stumble upon the church known locally as the Church of the Resurrection. It takes some finding but once located is a pearl of great price.

Containing the traditional sites of the death and resurrection of Jesus, this amazing building dates back originally to the fourth century. The austere Crusader façade is stunning, and entering the church quite daunting. The building has a mystique all its own. Layer upon layer of history are contained within its walls. Layer upon layer of faith pour out from its stonework. Alive with bright mosaics, exotic eastern liturgies and the smell of incense, generations of pilgrims have made the journey here to pray in the places where Jesus died and rose.

The Church of the Holy Sepulchre is the central shrine of Christendom with a long and fascinating history. It has played a significant part in the political events of the region and featured in many an international incident. It has been a place of prayer and devotion for sixteen centuries. Some of the early Christians soon saw this church as the "new temple" and the Tomb of Jesus as the new "Holy of Holies". For them, it was the place where God dwelt through the death and resurrection of Jesus.[36]

Today the church is shared by six different Christian denominations: Greek Orthodox, Armenian Orthodox, Roman Catholic or Latin, Syrian Orthodox, Coptic Orthodox and Ethiopian Orthodox. The church is often teeming with pilgrims and tourists, and finding a quiet place to pray can be difficult. The religious aura here is overpowering, and visitors can be overwhelmed. The stonework and glistening mosaics catch the imagination, and although there are numerous hidden corners and layers of the church waiting to be discovered, the two key focal points for us now are Calvary and the Tomb of Jesus.[37]

Calvary and the tomb

It was the Emperor Constantine the Great who first built a church here in the fourth century after the site had been excavated by his mother Helena. The story is told by Eusebius of Caesarea in his *Life of Constantine*, and there are several versions of the detail of the discovery of the true cross which was at one stage kept in the church.[38] Later writers tell of three crosses being found by Helena. They were laid upon sick people and the one that cured them was deemed to be the cross of Christ. A large basilica was constructed with its entrance up steps from the main street of Jerusalem. Beyond the entrance, pilgrims walked up a huge nave to the focal point of the building: a circular area containing the Tomb of Jesus consisting of a small octagonal structure in the style of a martyr's shrine. Constantine's Church of the Resurrection was dazzling and marked the beginning of the now centuries-long practice of Christian pilgrimage to the Holy Land. Sadly, this church was destroyed in the eleventh century although the Crusaders rebuilt it along the lines of a European gothic cathedral, and it flourished once again as a pilgrimage centre. It is largely the Crusader building that survives today with its spectacular entrance.

Just inside the church, up a flight of narrow stairs, is Calvary marked by two altars, one Roman Catholic and one Greek Orthodox. The Catholic one looks much as you would expect and has a mosaic of the crucifixion above it. The Orthodox altar, often less familiar to westerners, has larger-than-life figures of the crucifixion, the mother of Jesus and the beloved disciple. Silver and gold lamps bedeck the area. Around this altar, the bedrock of Calvary can be seen under glass, providing an important link back to the time of Jesus himself.

In the first century, Calvary was a quarry outside the city walls of Jerusalem. Mrs Alexander's famous hymn is wrong in that Calvary was never a "green hill far away" but right in that it was "without a city wall" meaning, of course, "outside" or "without" rather than "within" the walls. The city walls have changed several times since the first century and Calvary was brought inside the walls later in the first century. The modern walls are from the sixteenth century. And so, Jesus was crucified in a quarry outside Jerusalem's walls, a place where criminals were put to death by crucifixion, the Roman method of capital punishment.

Not far from Calvary in the Church of the Holy Sepulchre today, pilgrims visit the Tomb of Christ. In the early part of 2017 this was renovated by archaeologists.[39] But in any case, the modern structure looks quite different from the type of first-century tomb probably used for Jesus' burial. The "tomb" seen today is a nineteenth-century structure known as the "edicule" or "little house", an archaeological term for the tomb. It stands on the site where other structures commemorating the Tomb of Christ have stood, including the original Constantinian tomb from the fourth century. But the church and the tomb have been destroyed more than once, and it is unlikely that anything of the original Tomb of Christ remains where you see the nineteenth-century Tomb of Christ today.

However, nearby in a small chapel used by the Syrians some tombs from the time of Jesus can be seen. Indeed, this was a burial area and was originally, like the area of the crucifixion, outside the city wall and in the same quarry area as the crucifixion. As you peer through the darkness into these tombs, it is possible to discern niches where bodies would have been laid. And this gives a much better impression of what Jesus' burial might have looked like.

Even though Calvary and the Tomb of Jesus have changed in appearance over the centuries, they remain icons of Jesus' death and resurrection. They are focal places of prayer and devotion for thousands of Christians of many different denominations every year. But a visit to the Church of the Holy Sepulchre also raises some important and fascinating historical and theological questions: what do we really know about Jesus' death, burial and resurrection and what is their meaning for Christians now?

Crucifixion, burial and resurrection

All four Gospels tell us that Jesus died on a cross and was buried (Matthew 27:32–66; Mark 15:21–47; Luke 23:26–56; John 19:17–42). They also give us accounts of the empty tomb and the resurrection (Matthew 28; Mark 16; Luke 24; John 20–21). And Paul's writings are peppered with references to both (e.g. 1 Corinthians 1–2 and 15; Romans 4:25).

Crucifixion

First, the crucifixion. Thousands of people were crucified in the first century, and crucifixion was widely known. Jesus himself would have been familiar with it. There were different forms of crucifixion, including the one by which Jesus died. But the shape of the cross could be the other way up (the way the apostle Peter was crucified) or like an X (the way his brother Andrew was crucified) and sometimes with no shape at all. Hanging a dead person on a tree was familiar already in Judaism (Deuteronomy 21:21–23) and had a similar effect to crucifixion: it was a deterrent to other criminals who saw it.

Two other things are worth noting. Although we often think of Jesus being nailed to the cross through his hands, because that's how many crucifixes portray it, the nails probably went through the wrists. The palms of hands would easily have torn. Also, although in Christian imagination (largely reinforced by art) Jesus carried the whole cross to Calvary, in reality the criminal would have carried only the cross bar, while the upright beam would have been set in place in advance. Although popular films about Jesus' life and death portray him carrying the whole cross, this is very unlikely.

More important is the fact that death by crucifixion was a horrific death. It was reserved for common criminals, especially those who had committed treason or crime against the state. It was a death due to heart attack or asphyxiation. It was a painful and shameful method of torture which could last for days. The Gospels tell us that Jesus died relatively quickly. It was Passover in about 30 AD. John's Gospel tells us that they came to Jesus to break his legs (something that would mean the criminal would slump down on the cross and die quickly) but they found him already dead (19:31–33). Overall, we know quite a lot about crucifixion, and although the realities of this form of death might remain unimaginable for many of us, we can perhaps begin to envisage some of the horrors it involved.

Burial

But how would Jesus have been buried? In the first century there were several methods of Jewish burial. A lot depended on how wealthy you were. Most people were buried in mass graves. For the wealthy, however, there were several options. First, you could be buried on shelves like those seen in the catacombs in Rome. Or, you could be buried in a shallow trench grave—the method we are most familiar with in the west today. Or, you could be buried in what is known as a "rolling stone tomb". This was the most popular method in Judaea at the time of Jesus, and many examples have been discovered. Basically, this consisted of a tomb with a chamber at the front and several niches cut into the rock at the back. The body was prepared for burial in the chamber and then slid into a niche. The entrance to the chamber was then covered by a circular stone that rolled in a groove across the doorway, hence the name "rolling stone". About eighteen months after burial, the family of the deceased came back and scraped up the bones, gathered them together and put them into a box called an ossuary and then deposited that somewhere else. This is known as "secondary burial".

It is highly likely that Jesus of Nazareth was buried in a rolling stone tomb. The Gospels tell us that Joseph of Arimathea, a wealthy man, provided a new tomb (e.g. Matthew 27:57–60). The rolling stone type fits perfectly with what we know from the Gospels about Jesus' burial. And this is the type of tomb found in the Syrian chapel in the Church of the Holy Sepulchre. Jesus would have been taken into the chamber at the front of the grave and left there. The stone would then have been rolled over the entrance. But when the women went back after the sabbath with spices to anoint the body and complete the burial, he was gone.

Resurrection

As with the crucifixion, we can begin to envisage details of the burial of Jesus. But when we come to the resurrection a number of different problems arise.[40] Usually, popular discussions about the resurrection tend to get bogged down with the question of whether it really "happened". However, the broader context is also important and must always be kept in mind if we are to understand what the resurrection is all about. In the West, the resurrection has often been seen as an isolated event, whereas in the East the connection with the whole of humanity and with all creation has been appreciated much more.[41]

The Church of the Holy Sepulchre is known to locals as the Church of the Resurrection, emphasizing the importance of the resurrection, and this event has been central to Christian faith for two thousand years and is still so today. However, the church in Jerusalem, like the New Testament texts, doesn't tell us anything, as such, about the resurrection. There may be some hints, but both texts and building really just present us with an empty tomb. In fact, the important background for understanding the resurrection of Jesus comes from the Judaism of the time.

In the early layers of the Old Testament there is little indication of belief in resurrection or life after death. Ideas of "Sheol" as the place where the dead go can be found later as, for example, when Amos writes of God having power over Sheol (9:2), and therefore over death. And Job, in his attempts to come to terms with his sufferings, reflects that those who go down to Sheol do not come back up (7:9–10). The idea of bodily resurrection comes even later, especially in Ezekiel 37, although here the valley of dry bones indicates the whole nation of Israel rising and this is a corporate rather than an individual resurrection. The Book of Daniel, however, gives a clear indication that, "Many of those who sleep in the dust of the earth shall awake, some to everlasting life, and some to shame and everlasting contempt" (12:2).

Ideas developed further during the period between the Old and New Testaments, but there was no single view. We know that there were those such as the Sadducees who did not believe in resurrection. For those who did believe, resurrection involved both physical and spiritual dimensions. Overall, two things are crucial: first, in Jewish thinking, resurrection was something God did, and second, it was something corporate rather than individual. These aspects form the background to an appreciation of Jesus' resurrection then and now.

Cross and resurrection now

As Easter approaches and the crucifixion and resurrection of Jesus become the focus of our church services, so the final section of this book turns to their meaning today. I was once asked to give a talk on the question "Which is more important, the cross or the resurrection?" In a way, it was a misguided question, and my answer was, of course, that they are inseparable, two sides of a single coin. It is worth noting that in our church calendar and services, we separate Good Friday from Easter Day, treating them as commemorating different events. And cross and resurrection have often been separated in this way during all the centuries of theological reflection about them. But in the Gospels, the cross and resurrection clearly go together and are both part of the complete story of Jesus' life and God's purposes in it.

Part of the problem is that we usually hear only short readings of the Gospels and other New Testament texts in our churches today. We miss the overall sweep of the meaning of a single Gospel or letter. It always helps to read through a Gospel or letter completely, at one sitting. Then you get the wider context of meaning for all the parts in it. If you do that, you soon become aware that the crucifixion and resurrection are not just isolated events at the end of Jesus' life with no important background. In fact, they're part of the whole story of his life. Very often, even informed theological discussions of the meaning of the cross or resurrection concentrate on the single event torn away from its background. Believers and non-believers also often discuss the resurrection without reference to the life and death of Jesus. But Good Friday and Easter Day are part of a single event which is itself part of Jesus' whole life.

And so, it is the one who lived a life of teaching, preaching and healing who gets put to death and is raised. It is the one who tells parables and works miracles who gets put to death and is raised. It is the one who preaches and lives the ethics of the Sermon on the Mount who is put to death and is raised. And it is the one in whom God is seen in a new and challenging way and who provokes responses, who gets put to death and is raised.

In the gospel accounts the full story of Jesus comes to a climax in him being crucified and raised because of the life he lived. Jesus is put to death because of the things he stood for, even though there is wide discussion about what he might actually have been accused of under Roman or Jewish law. The Gospels vary in their accounts of the crucifixion and resurrection, bringing out different emphases and insights. All are clear, of course, that Jesus died on a Roman cross. But this was not the end. The empty tomb features in all four Gospels, and all Gospels (apart from the original version of Mark) have appearance stories as well: on a mountain in Galilee (Matthew 28:16–20), on the Road to Emmaus (Luke 24:13–35) and to Mary Magdalene in the Garden (John 20:11–18). It is clear in all this that the cross and resurrection go together and are the result of a particular life lived. They are all part of a continuous process.

This comes over with special poignancy in John's Gospel. Throughout this Gospel there are references to Jesus' coming death, to his "hour" coming (e.g. 2:4 and 7:30), and to him being "lifted up" (e.g. 8:28 and 12:32). Then, when the moment comes and Jesus is dying on the cross he cries out, "It is finished" (19:30) or "It is accomplished" (New English Bible), indicating that this is the moment when all his work comes to completion. It's as if the cross and the resurrection are one single event now played out on the cross. This sense is re-enforced when at the resurrection Jesus speaks of his ascension (20:17), thus emphasizing the overall continuity. For John, the sense is one of Jesus rising from the cross where death is overcome by resurrection in a single event. Death, resurrection and ascension are a continuous process in which death is turned into life.

For Paul also, cross and resurrection are profoundly intertwined. Although he talks about them on separate occasions, he clearly sees them as part of a continuum. The cross is fundamental to Paul's entire message, and the resurrection is God's own affirmation of everything Jesus has been and done. In Romans 5, Paul connects Christ to Adam and sees the whole human race as caught up with Jesus' crucifixion. The whole process is a corporate affair. In Romans 3:21–26, Paul is clear that the crucifixion is the event that changes the relation between God and the world. And in 1 Corinthians 15, he shows how in the resurrection God breathes new life into the whole of creation both physical and spiritual.[42] Paul's contribution is really important here: the overcoming of death and decay affects the entire creation and lifts everything, physical and spiritual, back to God. Again, the emphasis is on the resurrection as transforming death and decay.

There have been many interpretations of the crucifixion over the centuries. Focusing on the "Atonement" or "at-one-ment" (between God and humanity), some have seen it as a sacrifice, as a ransom or as a price paid to the devil. Some have seen it as a substitution, with Jesus satisfying God's justice by paying a price humanity could not pay.[43] There have been fewer "doctrines of the resurrection", but where there have been interpretations they have often been separated from the cross. The New Testament message is that in the resurrection of Jesus, God raises everything up towards himself, transforming pain and death into new life. Cross and resurrection, therefore, are not so much one event following another as one state of affairs turning into another: God's continuous action for the whole of creation. This is important in appreciating the overall meaning today.

So, which is more important, the cross or the resurrection? They are a single, continuous reality, part of God's purposes in creating and renewing creation and healing humanity. Part of the Jewish story of creation, Exodus, covenant and Passover, this single continuous event is rooted in the birth and life of Jesus of Nazareth, incorporating everything he lived for and stood for. Through his particular life of humility, compassion and self-giving, he became the dwelling place of God, the new temple (as we saw in week one of this book). He was killed for his innocent behaviour standing up for justice and peace. But God breathed new life into him, inaugurating the new covenant. The cross is the denial of selfishness; the resurrection is the new life that comes out of this and is God's victory over death.[44]

Conclusion

The Church of the Holy Sepulchre in Jerusalem has provided the lens through which we have looked at the death and resurrection of Jesus in this final chapter. We have visited Calvary and the tomb and have asked questions about the manner of Jesus' crucifixion and burial, and about the nature of his resurrection. We have also thought seriously about how to envisage their meaning today. It is clear that there have been many different ways of understanding these central aspects of Christian faith over the centuries and many metaphors have been used to bring out the various layers of meaning.

But there probably isn't a single explanation that captures everything about the death and resurrection of Jesus. We have emphasized them here as a continuous event revealing God's ways with the world: defeating evil, establishing new life through Jesus' self-giving and humility, and drawing us into that same way of life. God's presence breaks through in a new way in Jesus, offering his followers a new experience and a different style of living. And as disciples today we continue to face the challenge of living in the light of Jesus' life, death and resurrection. This entire process is what St Paul meant when he wrote of the "new creation" in Christ (Galatians 6:15).[45]

Things to do

Bible study passages
- Matthew 27:32–66; Mark 15:21–47; Luke 23:26–56
- John 20:11–18
- 1 Corinthians 15:1–11

Worship
- Psalms: 22; 66:1–11; 117
- Hymns: O sacred head, surrounded; Thine be the glory.

Activities

- Visit your local church to see what symbols are used on Good Friday and Easter Day.
- Look for signs of dying and rising in life and nature.

Questions for discussion

- What do we know about the crucifixion and burial of Jesus?
- Was Jesus' death a victory or a defeat?
- How should Christians today understand the resurrection?

Further reading

Paula Gooder, *Journey to the Empty Tomb* (Norwich: Canterbury Press, 2014).

Graham Tomlin, *Looking Through the Cross* (London: Bloomsbury, 2013).

Rowan Williams, *God with Us: The Meaning of the Cross and Resurrection Then and Now* (London: SPCK, 2017).

Afterword

In this book I have attempted to open up a view of Jesus and the Christian life through week-by-week study and discussion sessions designed for the seasons of Advent and Lent. Using lenses from the Holy Land alongside gospel texts to stimulate the imagination, the overall picture that has emerged from this "armchair pilgrimage" now looks something like this: we can think of Jesus in the same light as ancient Jews thought of their temple in Jerusalem. He is the place where God dwells. His life, death and resurrection show us that God can be found in him in a particular way. It was in Jesus that God "stooped" to dwell and in his lifestyle people saw new things about God. We were reminded of this stooping of God in Jesus by the Church of the Nativity in Bethlehem and the concept has had a special place in New Testament and Christian theological thinking from the very beginning.

From Nazareth we learnt that Jesus was "wise" and was in this respect close to God's purposes. This indicated that we too can become wise if we follow his ways. Finally, in the first section, at the River Jordan, Jesus emerged as one who committed himself to God's purposes and chose God rather than the many other alternatives. We can do the same. Overall, through the four weeks of Advent, a picture emerged of God dwelling in Jesus, and of our basic responses as Christians.

In the second section of the book, designed for Lent, further detail was added to this basic picture. Jesus' encounter with the devil in the desert led to reflection on what Christians can gain from a desert experience. Once again, the experience of the presence of God led to a sense of response. From Galilee there emerged Jesus the teacher, preacher and healer and his message of the kingdom of God, a message that again draws us in and demands an appropriate lifestyle in response. Caesarea Philippi was the great divider, however, challenging disciples to make the ultimate decision to follow Jesus or not. The transfiguration at Mount

Tabor was a special moment revealing the distinctive presence of Jesus leading on to the possible transfiguration of the world through Christian discipleship. The Last Supper and the death and resurrection of Jesus in Jerusalem brought out the same dynamic: Jesus' presence draws us in and our response can lead to new life.

In all of this, through the use of a series of lenses from the Holy Land and through study of associated texts from the four Gospels in the New Testament, these ten chapters should have moulded for you a sense of a very real, human Jesus whose life, death and resurrection show us something fundamental about God's ways with the world. They have portrayed a Jesus who reveals God in particular ways and whose example offers Christians a different way of being in the world. I hope you have found this book useful, stimulating and above all inspiring for faith and life lived in Jesus' name.

Notes

1   If you want more background see Peter Walker, *In the Steps of Jesus: An Illustrated Guide to the Places of the Holy Land* (Oxford: Lion, 2nd ed., 2018); and Jerome Murphy-O'Connor, *The Holy Land: An Oxford Archaeological Guide* (Oxford: Oxford University Press, 2008). See also James Martin, *Jesus: A Pilgrimage* (New York: HarperCollins, 2016).

2   See Josephus, *The Jewish War*, trans. G. A. Williamson, ed. E. Mary Smallwood (London: Penguin, 1981), p. 304.

3   For a full account, see Josephus, *The Jewish War*, chapters 17–23.

4   Margaret Barker, *The Gate of Heaven: The History and Symbolism of the Temple in Jerusalem* (London: SPCK, 1991). Margaret Barker has developed a detailed and fascinating "temple theology" focusing mostly on the First Temple in Jerusalem and its influence on the New Testament and other writings. See her *Temple Theology: An Introduction* (London: SPCK, 2004).

5   For a scholarly discussion of the options, see E. P. Sanders, *Jesus and Judaism* (London: SCM, 1985), Part One.

6   For further study of the Jerusalem Temple and its importance in reading the New Testament, see the two books by Nicholas Perrin: *Jesus the Temple* (London: SPCK, 2010), and *Jesus the Priest* (London: SPCK, 2018).

7   For a stimulating discussion of finding God in different landscapes, see Graham B. Usher, *Places of Enchantment: Meeting God in Landscapes* (London: SPCK, 2012).

8   For a useful discussion of some of the elements of the gospel picture of Jesus that might go back to him, and of the different New Testament portrayals of him, see James D. G. Dunn, *Jesus According to the New Testament* (Grand Rapids: Eerdmans, 2019).

9   Though see John 7:42 where there is reference to the Messiah coming from Bethlehem.

10 The classic study of the birth narratives in Matthew and Luke is Raymond E. Brown, *The Birth of the Messiah: A Commentary on the Infancy Narratives*

in Matthew and Luke (London: Cassell, 1993). For a view that sees the birth stories in the context of the Jerusalem Temple and its traditions, see Margaret Barker, *Christmas: The Original Story* (London: SPCK, 2008).

[11] For an introduction to the apocryphal Gospels, see Paul Foster, *The Apocryphal Gospels: A Very Short Introduction* (Oxford: Oxford University Press, 2009). For the texts of the later Gospels, see J. K. Elliott, *The Apocryphal New Testament* (Oxford: Clarendon, 1993).

[12] See e.g. *The Infancy Gospel of Thomas* in J. K. Elliott, *The Apocryphal New Testament* (Oxford: Clarendon, 1993), pp. 68–83.

[13] For a thorough, scholarly study of this idea, see Ben Witherington III, *Jesus the Sage: The Pilgrimage of Wisdom* (Minneapolis, MN: Augsburg Fortress, 1994).

[14] For a contemporary interpretation, see Katherine Dell, *Seeking a Life that Matters: Wisdom for Today from the Book of Proverbs* (London: DLT, 2002).

[15] A good place to begin this process is with Martin Laird, *Into the Silent Land: The Practice of Contemplation* (London: DLT, 2006). See also his *A Sunlit Absence: Silence, Awareness and Contemplation* (Oxford: Oxford University Press, 2011) and *An Ocean of Light: Contemplation, Transformation and Liberation* (New York: Oxford University Press, 2019).

[16] For a fuller working-out of this idea, see the now classic work by John Austin Baker, *The Foolishness of God* (London: DLT, 1970).

[17] For more on living wisely, see David F. Ford, *The Drama of Living: Being Wise in the Spirit* (Norwich: Canterbury Press, 2014).

[18] For a fascinating account of the traditions relating to John the Baptist and the story of the discovery of a cave in the Holy Land allegedly associated with him, see Shimon Gibson, *The Cave of John the Baptist: The First Archaeological Evidence of the Historical Reality of the Gospel Story* (London: Century, 2004).

[19] See Josephus, *Antiquities of the Jews*, xviii. v. 2 in *The New Complete Works of Josephus*, trans. William Whiston (Grand Rapids, MI: Kregel, 1999).

[20] For an account of this development, see Derwas A. Chitty, *The Desert a City: An Introduction to the Study of Egyptian and Palestinian Monasticism under the Christian Empire* (New York: SVS Press, 1977); and also John Binns (ed.), *Cyril of Scythopolis: The Lives of the Monks of Palestine* (Collegeville, MN: Cistercian Publications, 1991). Some of the sayings of the desert fathers can be found in Benedicta Ward, *The Desert Fathers: Sayings of the Early Christian Monks* (London: Penguin, 2003).

21 See Athanasius, *Life of St Antony,* available at <http://www.fordham.edu/halsall/sbook.html>.

22 The *lavra* or *laura* was the lane or alleyway of cells under the supervision of a superior.

23 For a lively and imaginative portrayal of Abraham and his significance for Jews, Christians and Muslims, see Bruce Feiler, *Abraham: A Journey to the Heart of Three Faiths* (New York: HarperCollins, 2002).

24 For one example of a response to the temptations of wealth, see Justin Welby, *Dethroning Mammon: Making Money Serve Grace* (London: Bloomsbury, 2016).

25 The "process" philosopher A. N. Whitehead wrote of Jesus' "brief Galilean vision of humility . . . " in *Process and Reality: An Essay in Cosmology* (London: Macmillan, 1978), p. 342.

26 For further study of the historical Jesus and his legacy see Richard Bauckham, *Jesus: A Very Short Introduction* (Oxford: Oxford University Press, 2011); Helen Bond, *Jesus: A Very Brief History* (London: SPCK, 2017); Ed Kessler, *Jesus* (Stroud: The History Press, 2016); and Peter Walker, *Jesus and His World* (Oxford: Lion, 2003).

27 For a short introduction to the Lord's Prayer, see Tom Wright, *The Lord and His Prayer* (London: SPCK, 1996).

28 For a thorough literary and theological study of the sermon, see Jonathan T. Pennington, *The Sermon on the Mount and Human Flourishing* (Grand Rapids, MI: Baker, 2017).

29 This is Paul Tillich's suggestion in *Systematic Theology* Vol 2 Part III *Existence and the Christ* (London: SCM Press, 1978), pp. 97f.

30 See Dietrich Bonhoeffer, *Letters and Papers from Prison,* ed. Eberhard Bethge (London: SCM Press, 2001), p. 91.

31 For further reflection on the life of Christian disciples, see Rowan Williams, *Being Disciples: Essentials of the Christian Life* (London: SPCK, 2016).

32 A useful introduction is Martin Bunton, *The Palestinian–Israeli Conflict: A Very Short Introduction* (Oxford: Oxford University Press, 2013).

33 For a classic study of the meaning of the transfiguration of Jesus, see Arthur Michael Ramsey, *The Glory of God and the Transfiguration of Christ* (Eugene, OR: Wipf and Stock, 2009).

34 See 'A Catechism' in the Church of England's *The Book of Common Prayer* of 1662.

35 For a rich and rewarding exposition of the Eucharist today, see Timothy Radcliffe, *Why Go to Church? The Drama of the Eucharist* (London: Continuum, 2008).

36 For a lively and interesting illustrated study of the Jewish temples and their influence on later Jewish, Christian and Muslim art, architecture and theology, see William J. Hamblin and David Rolph Seely, *Solomon's Temple: Myth and History* (London: Thames & Hudson, 2007).

37 For a short, illustrated introduction and guided tour of the church, see Stephen W. Need, *Jerusalem. The Church of the Holy Sepulchre: An Introduction and Guide* (Jerusalem: Carta, 2016).

38 See Eusebius of Caesarea, *Life of Constantine,* available at <http://www.fordham.edu/halsall/sbook.html>.

39 For a very interesting and comprehensive illustrated archaeological history of the Tomb of Christ, see Martin Biddle, *The Tomb of Christ* (Stroud: Sutton, 1999). See also Kristin Romey, "The Search for the Real Jesus", *National Geographic*, December 2017, pp. 30–69.

40 For a wide-ranging and accessible study of some of the literary, historical and theological dimensions of the resurrection, see Lidija Novakovic, *Resurrection: A Guide for the Perplexed* (London: Bloomsbury T&T Clark, 2016).

41 For a lively and colourful exploration of the differences, see John Dominic Crossan and Sarah Sexton Crossan, *Resurrecting Easter: How the West Lost and the East Kept the Original Easter Vision* (New York: HarperCollins, 2018).

42 For a study that takes the thoughts in this section much further, see Frances Young, *Construing the Cross: Type, Sign, Symbol, Word, Action* (London: SPCK, 2016).

43 For accounts of the meaning of the crucifixion, see Gustav Aulén, *Christus Victor: An Historical Study of the Three Main Types of the Idea of the Atonement* (London: SPCK, 2010) and the famous work by the scholastic philosopher and theologian Anselm of Canterbury (1033–1109), *Cur Deus Homo* (Why God Became a Human Being), available at <http://www.fordham.edu/halsall/sbook.html>.

44 For more on the resurrection and its meaning for Christian living, see Paula Gooder, *This Risen Existence: The Spirit of Easter* (Norwich: Canterbury Press, 2009) and Rowan Williams, *Resurrection: Interpreting the Easter Gospel* (London: DLT, 2014).

45   For further exploration of some of the issues raised in this chapter, see N. T. Wright, *The Day the Revolution Began: Reconsidering the Meaning of Jesus's Crucifixion* (New York: HarperOne, 2018).

EU GPSR Authorized Representative:

LOGOS EUROPE, 9 rue Nicolas Poussin, 17000 La Rochelle, France

contact@logoseurope.eu

www.ingramcontent.com/pod-product-compliance
Lightning Source LLC
Chambersburg PA
CBHW060438090426
42733CB00011B/2322